지은이	NE능률 영어교육연구소
선임연구원	김지현
연구원	송민아, 김준희
영문교열	Curtis Thompson, Angela Lan, Olk Bryce Barrett
디자인	안훈정
내지 일러스트	김주명, 곽호명, 박응식
맥편집	권재희

Photo Credits   Shutterstock

NE능률이
미래를
창조합니다.

건강한 배움의 고객가치를 제공하겠다는 꿈을 실현하기 위해
40년이 넘는 시간 동안 열심히 달려왔습니다.

앞으로도 끊임없는 연구와 노력을 통해
당연한 것을 멈추지 않고

고객, 기업, 직원 모두가 함께 성장하는 NE능률이 되겠습니다.

초등
Grammar
Inside

2

# 구성 및 활용법

| STEP 1 | 문법 개념 확인 | ▶ | STEP 2 | 연습 문제 |

STEP 1 — 문법 개념 확인
쉽고 간단한 문법 설명과 시각적으로 잘 정리된 표를 통해 문법 개념을 빠르게 익혀요.

STEP 2 — 연습 문제
간단한 확인 문제부터 문장 완성까지 다양한 유형과 난이도의 문제로 배운 문법을 적용해요.

① 학습목표
해당 Chapter에서 배울 내용을 미리 예측해 볼 수 있어요.

② WORD CHECK
Chapter에 등장할 단어를 미리 학습할 수 있어요.

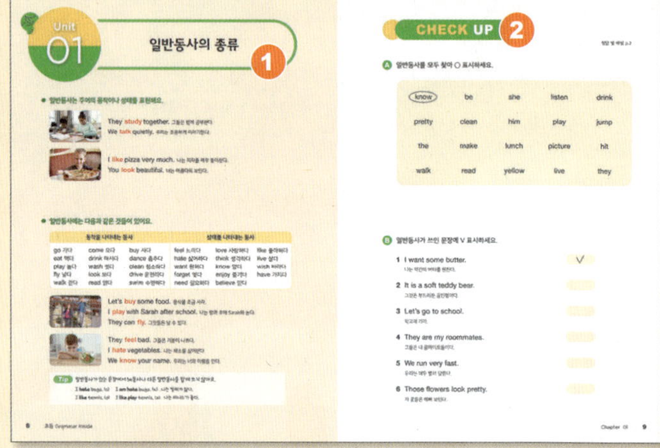

① 문법 설명
한눈에 들어오는 문법 설명과 예문으로 문법 개념을 쉽게 이해할 수 있어요.

② CHECK UP
단순한 고르기 문제를 통해 문법 개념을 제대로 이해했는지 확인할 수 있어요.

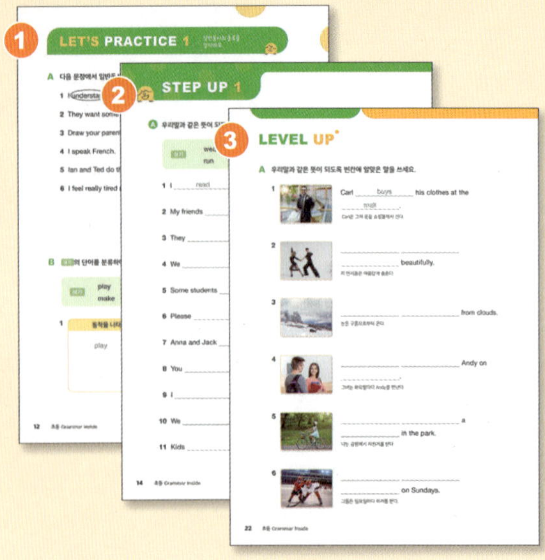

① LET'S PRACTICE
간단한 유형의 문제로 새로 학습한 내용을 충분히 이해했는지 점검할 수 있어요.

② STEP UP
빈칸 채우기부터 통문장 완성까지 다양한 유형의 문제를 풀어보며 문법 포인트를 확실히 익힐 수 있어요.

③ LEVEL UP
빈칸 채우기 활동으로 앞서 학습한 문장을 다시 써보고 문법 개념을 정확히 학습했는지 파악할 수 있어요.

실제 교내 평가 유형의 챕터 REVIEW TEST,
실전 Test, 총괄평가로 앞에서 배운 문법 내용을
복습해요.

본책에 쓰인 문장을 그대로 활용한 추가 문제를
풀어 보며 문법 개념을 제대로 익혔는지 확인해요.

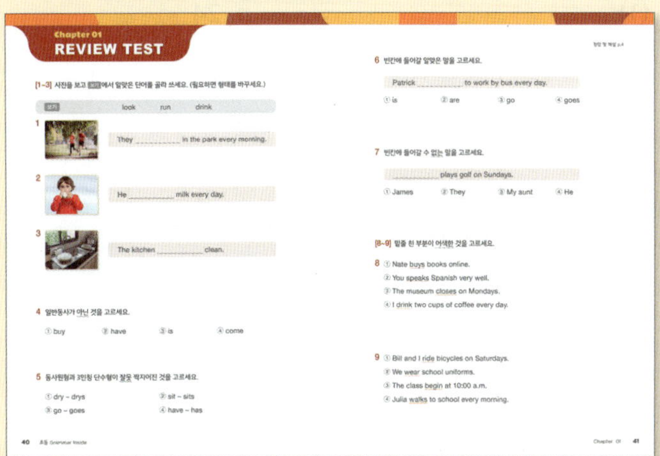

REVIEW TEST

다양한 유형의 객관식 문제와 서술형 문제를 통해 해당
챕터에서 배운 내용을 정리해볼 수 있어요.

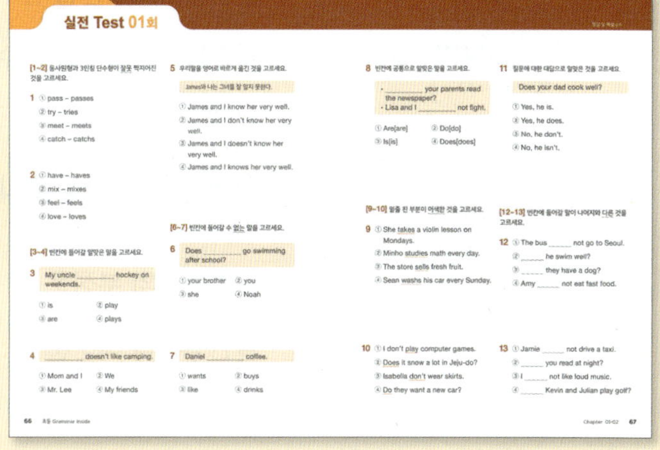

실전 Test

두 개의 챕터를 학습 후에는 실제 교내 평가 유형의 문제를
통해 지금까지 배운 내용을 다시 상기할 수 있어요.

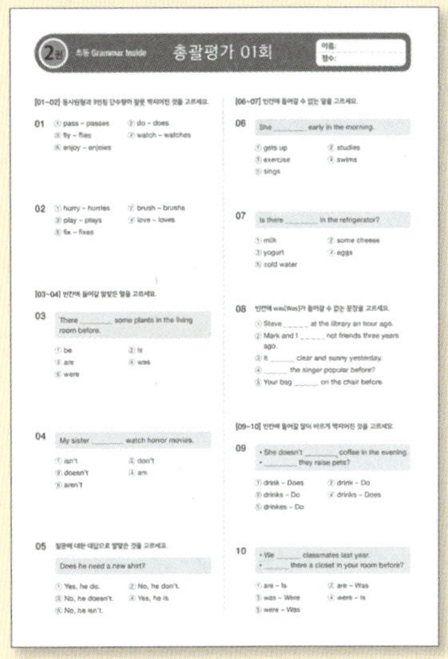

총괄평가

총 2회의 총괄평가를 통해 책 전체의
내용을 복습할 수 있어요.

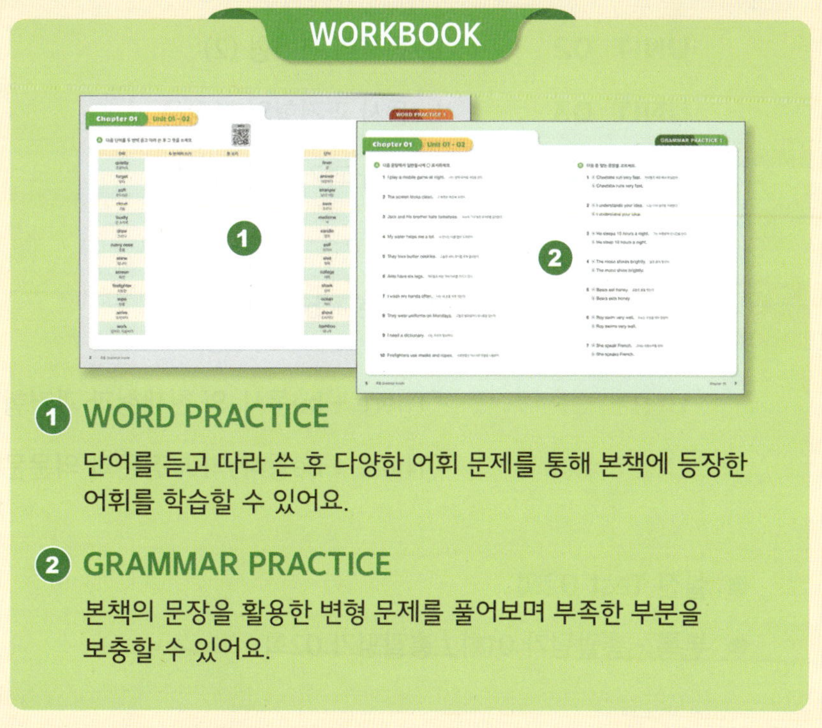

1 WORD PRACTICE

단어를 듣고 따라 쓴 후 다양한 어휘 문제를 통해 본책에 등장한
어휘를 학습할 수 있어요.

2 GRAMMAR PRACTICE

본책의 문장을 활용한 변형 문제를 풀어보며 부족한 부분을
보충할 수 있어요.

목차

20일 학습플랜

하루에 본책 두 개의 Unit을 학습하고 워크북으로 복습하는 구성입니다.
워크북을 수업에 활용 시 **32차시** 수업이 가능합니다.

차시	학습 내용		숙제	학습 날짜	
1 차시	CHAPTER 01 UNIT 01 - 02	CHECK UP LET'S PRACTICE 1~2	워크북 CH 01 UNIT 01~02	월	일
2 차시		STEP UP 1~4 LEVEL UP		월	일
3 차시	CHAPTER 01 UNIT 03 - 04	CHECK UP LET'S PRACTICE 1~2	워크북 CH 01 UNIT 03~04	월	일
4 차시		STEP UP 1~4 LEVEL UP		월	일
5 차시	CHAPTER 01	REVIEW TEST		월	일
6 차시	CHAPTER 02 UNIT 01 - 02	CHECK UP LET'S PRACTICE 1~2	워크북 CH 02 UNIT 01~02	월	일
7 차시		STEP UP 1~4 LEVEL UP		월	일
8 차시	CHAPTER 02	REVIEW TEST		월	일
9 차시	실전 Test 01회			월	일
10 차시	CHAPTER 03 UNIT 01 - 02	CHECK UP LET'S PRACTICE 1~2	워크북 CH 03 UNIT 01~02	월	일
11 차시		STEP UP 1~4 LEVEL UP		월	일
12 차시	CHAPTER 03 UNIT 03 - 04	CHECK UP LET'S PRACTICE 1~2	워크북 CH 03 UNIT 03~04	월	일
13 차시		STEP UP 1~4 LEVEL UP		월	일
14 차시	CHAPTER 03	REVIEW TEST		월	일
15 차시	CHAPTER 04 UNIT 01 - 02	CHECK UP LET'S PRACTICE 1~2	워크북 CH 04 UNIT 01~02	월	일
16 차시		STEP UP 1~4 LEVEL UP		월	일
17 차시	CHAPTER 04	REVIEW TEST		월	일
18 차시	실전 Test 02회			월	일
19 차시	총괄평가 01회			월	일
20 차시	총괄평가 02회			월	일

일반동사

학습목표

1 일반동사의 종류에 대해 알아보아요.
2 일반동사 현재형의 쓰임을 알아보아요.
3 일반동사 3인칭 단수형의 규칙 변화를 알아보아요.
4 일반동사 3인칭 단수형의 불규칙 변화를 알아보아요.

WORD CHECK

forget
잊다

cloud
구름

screen
화면

rope
밧줄

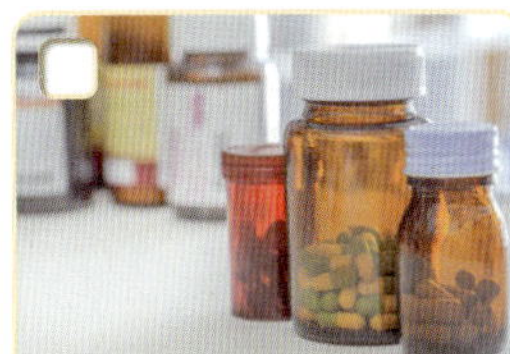

medicine
약

candle
양초

pull
당기다

shark
상어

shout
소리치다

bamboo
대나무

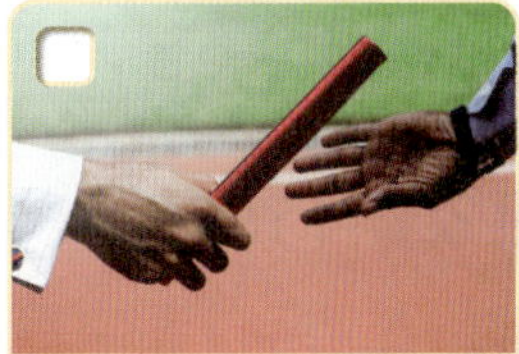

pass
건네주다

fix
고치다

shoulder
어깨

tail
꼬리

feed
밥을 먹이다

watermelon
수박

gym
체육관

swan
백조

piggy bank
돼지 저금통

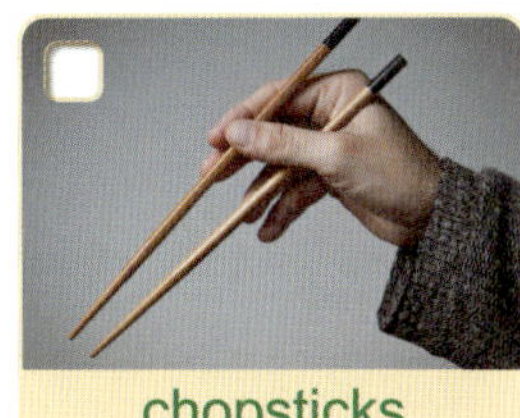

chopsticks
젓가락

일반동사의 종류

● **일반동사는 주어의 동작이나 상태를 표현해요.**

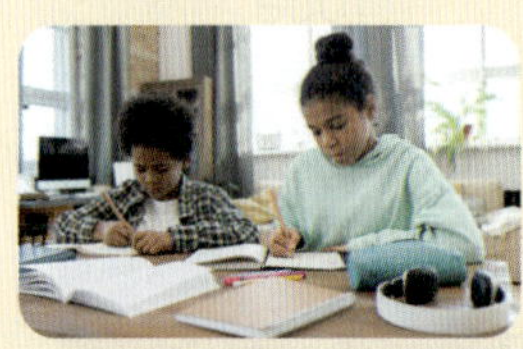

They **study** together. 그들은 함께 공부한다.
We **talk** quietly. 우리는 조용하게 이야기한다.

I **like** pizza very much. 나는 피자를 매우 좋아한다.
You **look** beautiful. 너는 아름다워 보인다.

● **일반동사에는 다음과 같은 것들이 있어요.**

동작을 나타내는 동사			상태를 나타내는 동사		
go 가다	come 오다	buy 사다	feel 느끼다	love 사랑하다	like 좋아하다
eat 먹다	drink 마시다	dance 춤추다	hate 싫어하다	think 생각하다	live 살다
play 놀다	wash 씻다	clean 청소하다	want 원하다	know 알다	wish 바라다
fly 날다	look 보다	drive 운전하다	forget 잊다	enjoy 즐기다	have 가지다
walk 걷다	read 읽다	swim 수영하다	need 필요하다	believe 믿다	

Let's **buy** some food. 음식을 조금 사자.
I **play** with Sarah after school. 나는 방과 후에 Sarah와 논다.
They can **fly**. 그것들은 날 수 있다.

They **feel** bad. 그들은 기분이 나쁘다.
I **hate** vegetables. 나는 채소를 싫어한다.
We **know** your name. 우리는 너의 이름을 안다.

> **Tip** 일반동사가 있는 문장에서 be동사나 다른 일반동사를 함께 쓰지 않아요.
> I **hate** bugs. (o)　　I **am hate** bugs. (x)　나는 벌레가 싫다.
> I **like** tennis. (o)　　I **like play** tennis. (x)　나는 테니스가 좋다.

CHECK UP

A 일반동사를 모두 찾아 ○ 표시하세요.

know	be	she	listen	drink
pretty	clean	him	play	jump
the	make	lunch	picture	hit
walk	read	yellow	live	they

B 일반동사가 쓰인 문장에 V 표시하세요.

1 I want some butter.
나는 약간의 버터를 원한다.

2 It is a soft teddy bear.
그것은 부드러운 곰인형이다.

3 Let's go to school.
학교에 가자.

4 They are my roommates.
그들은 내 룸메이트들이다.

5 We run very fast.
우리는 매우 빨리 달린다.

6 Those flowers look pretty.
저 꽃들은 예뻐 보인다.

일반동사의 현재형

- **일반동사의 현재형은 현재의 상태 또는 일어나고 있는 일을 나타내요.**

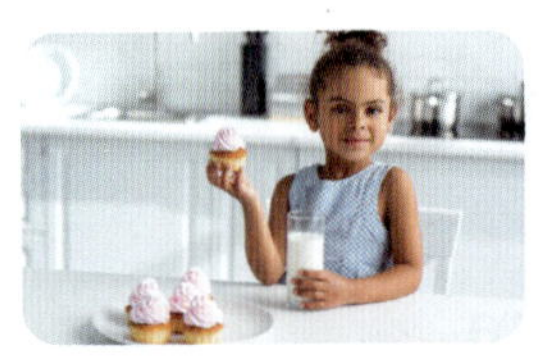

I **have** cupcakes. 나는 컵케이크들을 가지고 있다.

They **feel** angry now. 그들은 지금 화가 난다.

She **needs** a piece of paper. 그녀는 종이 한 장이 필요하다.

Tip 주어가 3인칭 단수일 때는 보통 동사원형에 -s를 붙여서 현재형을 만들어요.

Eva love**s** her family. Eva는 그녀의 가족을 사랑한다.

This cookie smell**s** good. 이 쿠키는 냄새가 좋다.

- **현재 일어나고 있는 일 외에도, 다음의 경우 현재시제를 써요.**

반복되는 습관을 나타낼 때		I **play** soccer every day. 나는 매일 축구를 한다. Anna **drinks** coffee every morning. Anna는 매일 아침 커피를 마신다.
일반적/과학적 사실을 나타낼 때		Americans **speak** English. 미국인들은 영어로 말한다. The earth **moves** around the sun. 지구는 태양 주위에서 움직인다. Snow **comes** from clouds. 눈은 구름으로부터 온다.

Tip 반복되는 습관을 나타낼 때는 다음 표현을 자주 사용해요.

every day 매일   every morning 매일 아침   on Sundays 일요일마다

I play basketball with my friends **on Sundays**. 나는 일요일마다 내 친구들과 함께 농구를 한다.

CHECK UP

A 다음 문장에서 일반동사에 ○ 표시하고 알맞은 현재시제의 쓰임에 V 표시하세요.

	현재의 상태	반복되는 습관	일반적 사실
1 Cheetahs (run) very fast.	☐	☐	✔
2 I need a dictionary.	☐	☐	☐
3 They love butter cookies.	☐	☐	☐
4 I wash my hands often.	☐	☐	☐
5 Ants have six legs.	☐	☐	☐

B ( ) 안에서 알맞은 것을 고르세요.

1 
I (walk / walks) my dog every day.
나는 매일 나의 개를 산책시킨다.

2 
Lemons (taste / tastes) sour.
레몬들은 신맛이 난다.

3 
They (sing / sings) so loudly.
그들은 매우 큰 소리로 노래한다.

4 
Roy (swim / swims) very well.
Roy는 수영을 매우 잘한다.

A 다음 문장에서 일반동사에 ○ 표시하세요.

1 I (understand) your idea. 나는 너의 생각을 이해한다.

2 They want some milk. 그들은 우유를 조금 원한다.

3 Draw your parents. 너의 부모님을 그려라.

4 I speak French. 나는 프랑스어를 한다.

5 Ian and Ted do their homework every day. Ian과 Ted는 매일 숙제를 한다.

6 I feel really tired right now. 나는 지금 정말 피곤하다.

B 보기 의 단어를 분류하여 쓰세요.

| 보기 | play | drink | know | run | hate |
| | make | feel | talk | love | think |

1 동작을 나타내는 동사	**2** 상태를 나타내는 동사
play	

LET'S PRACTICE 2 

일반동사의 현재형을 연습해요.

A ( ) 안에서 알맞은 것을 고르세요.

1 I (am / have) a runny nose.　나는 콧물이 난다.

2 They (are / brush) their teeth every day.　그들은 매일 이를 닦는다.

3 This book (is / buys) expensive.　이 책은 비싸다.

4 Bears (are / eat) honey.　곰들은 꿀을 먹는다.

5 My brothers (are / make) twins.　내 오빠들은 쌍둥이이다.

6 The moon (is / shines) brightly.　달은 밝게 빛난다.

B 밑줄 친 부분을 바르게 고쳐 쓰세요.

1 I plays a mobile game at night.　➡　play
나는 밤에 모바일 게임을 한다.

2 The screen look clean.　➡　________
그 화면은 깨끗해 보인다.

3 My sister help me a lot.　➡　________
내 언니는 나를 많이 도와준다.

4 They wears uniforms on Mondays.　➡　________
그들은 월요일마다 유니폼을 입는다.

5 Jack and his brother hates tomatoes.　➡　________
Jack과 그의 형은 토마토를 싫어한다.

6 Firefighters uses masks and ropes.　➡　________
소방관들은 마스크와 밧줄을 사용한다.

A 우리말과 같은 뜻이 되도록 보기 에서 알맞은 말을 골라 쓰세요.

보기					
wear	take	enjoy	get up	use	love
run	read	come	go	learn	

1 I _______read_______ two books a day. 나는 하루에 두 권의 책을 읽는다.

2 My friends _______________ playing tennis. 내 친구들은 테니스 치는 것을 즐긴다.

3 They _______________ to school by bus. 그들은 버스를 타고 학교에 간다.

4 We _______________ early in the morning. 우리는 아침에 일찍 일어난다.

5 Some students _______________ history. 몇 명의 학생들은 역사를 배운다.

6 Please _______________ to our party. 우리의 파티에 오세요.

7 Anna and Jack _______________ fast. Anna와 Jack은 빠르게 달린다.

8 You _______________ too much water. 너는 너무 많은 물을 쓴다.

9 I _______________ a guitar class on Fridays. 나는 금요일마다 기타 수업을 듣는다.

10 We _______________ our parents. 우리는 우리의 부모님을 사랑한다.

11 Kids _______________ heavy helmets. 아이들은 무거운 헬멧을 쓴다.

B 밑줄 친 동사를 현재형으로 알맞게 고쳐 쓰세요.

1 Frogs <u>sleeps</u> during winter.   →   _______sleep_______
개구리들은 겨울 동안 잠을 잔다.

2 I <u>likes</u> my tablet PC.   →   _______________
나는 내 태블릿 PC를 좋아한다.

3 This tree <u>grow</u> so fast.   →   _______________
이 나무는 아주 빠르게 자란다.

4 They <u>knows</u> it very well.   →   _______________
그들은 그것을 매우 잘 안다.

5 The subway <u>arrive</u> at 3:00 p.m.   →   _______________
그 지하철은 오후 3시에 도착한다.

6 Those dancers <u>dances</u> beautifully.   →   _______________
저 댄서들은 아름답게 춤춘다.

7 Your voice <u>sound</u> so soft.   →   _______________
너의 목소리는 아주 부드럽게 들린다.

8 Tom and Meg <u>works</u> at the library.   →   _______________
Tom과 Meg는 도서관에서 일한다.

9 We <u>writes</u> a novel together.   →   _______________
우리는 함께 소설을 쓴다.

10 They <u>plays</u> hockey on Sundays.   →   _______________
그들은 일요일마다 하키를 한다.

11 I <u>rides</u> a bike in the park.   →   _______________
나는 공원에서 자전거를 탄다.

12 Hanna <u>hate</u> coffee.   →   _______________
Hanna는 커피를 싫어한다.

A 사진을 보고 주어진 말을 이용하여 빈칸에 알맞은 말을 쓰세요.

1 

I _______have_______ a fever. (have)

나는 열이 있다.

2 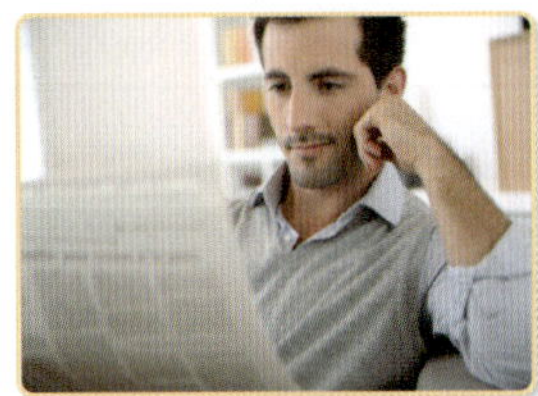

My father _______________ the newspaper every morning. (read)

내 아버지는 매일 아침 신문을 읽으신다.

3 

Monkeys _______________ bananas. (eat)

원숭이들은 바나나를 먹는다.

4 

The birds _______________ to the west. (fly)

새들은 서쪽으로 날아간다.

5 

This mirror _______________ so dirty. (look)

이 거울은 아주 더러워 보인다.

6 

He _______________ 10 hours a night. (sleep)

그는 하룻밤에 10시간을 잔다.

Ⓑ 우리말과 같은 뜻이 되도록 [보기]에서 알맞은 단어를 골라 쓰세요. (필요하면 형태를 바꾸세요.)

보기	need	feel	like	help	shine	drive
	dry	meet	answer	hate	bake	

1 I ________dry________ my hair every day. 나는 매일 내 머리를 말린다.

2 She ________________ Andy on Tuesdays. 그녀는 화요일마다 Andy를 만난다.

3 We ________________ our parents a lot. 우리는 우리의 부모님을 많이 도와드린다.

4 Bora always ________________ quickly. 보라는 항상 빠르게 대답한다.

5 The stars ________________ so brightly. 별들이 매우 밝게 빛난다.

6 I ________________ really sorry for him. 나는 그가 매우 안쓰럽다고 느낀다.

7 Cindy ________________ some pepper. Cindy는 후추가 조금 필요하다.

8 Bakers ________________ bread every morning. 제빵사들은 매일 아침 빵을 굽는다.

9 He ________________ action movies. 그는 액션 영화를 좋아한다.

10 They ________________ very well. 그들은 운전을 매우 잘한다.

11 My cat ________________ strangers. 내 고양이는 낯선 사람을 싫어한다.

STEP UP 3

A 주어진 동사를 빈칸에 알맞은 현재형으로 쓰세요.

1 I _____clean_____ my room every day. (clean) 나는 매일 내 방을 청소한다.

She _____cleans_____ the floor alone. 그녀는 혼자서 바닥을 청소한다.

2 We _____________ exercising. (love) 우리는 운동하는 것을 매우 좋아한다.

Josh _____________ doing yoga. Josh는 요가하는 것을 매우 좋아한다.

3 He _____________ orange juice. (want) 그는 오렌지 주스를 원한다.

They _____________ some tea. 그들은 약간의 차를 원한다.

4 Firefighters _____________ many lives. (save) 소방관들은 많은 생명을 구한다.

This medicine _____________ people's lives. 이 약이 사람들의 생명을 구한다.

5 Carl _____________ his clothes at the mall. (buy) Carl은 그의 옷을 쇼핑몰에서 산다.

You always _____________ nice clothes. 너는 항상 좋은 옷을 산다.

6 The cake _____________ so delicious. (smell) 이 케이크는 아주 맛있는 냄새가 난다.

Those candles _____________ very good. 저 양초들은 냄새가 매우 좋다.

7 Elephants _____________ the cart. (pull) 코끼리들은 수레를 끈다.

The boy _____________ the sled. 그 소년이 썰매를 끈다.

8 They _____________ the zoo very often. (visit) 그들은 동물원을 매우 자주 방문한다.

He _____________ his uncle every summer. 그는 매년 여름 그의 삼촌댁을 방문한다.

B 우리말과 같은 뜻이 되도록 주어진 말을 이용하여 문장을 완성하세요.

1 나는 너의 메시지를 이해한다. (understand)

→ __________ I __________ __________ understand __________ your message.

2 그녀는 요즘에 영어를 배운다. (learn)

→ __________________ __________________ English these days.

3 우리는 대학에 간다. (go)

→ __________________ __________________ to our college.

4 Kate는 그를 위해 편지를 쓴다. (write)

→ __________________ __________________ a letter for him.

5 그들은 많이 먹는다. (eat)

→ __________________ __________________ a lot.

6 Harry는 로봇들을 가지고 논다. (play)

→ __________________ __________________ with robots.

7 나는 내 조부모님이 그립다. (miss)

→ __________________ __________________ my grandparents.

8 상어들은 바다에 산다. (live in)

→ Sharks __________________ __________________ the ocean.

9 나는 외로움을 느낀다. (feel)

→ __________________ __________________ lonely.

10 그는 매일 사진들을 찍는다. (take)

→ __________________ __________________ photos every day.

STEP UP 4

A 다음 문장을 주어진 주어로 시작하는 문장으로 바꿔 쓰세요.

1 They want a smartphone. 그들은 스마트폰을 원한다.

→ Angela _______ wants a smartphone _______.

2 She cooks dinner every day. 그녀는 매일 저녁 식사를 요리한다.

→ I _______.

3 The speakers work well. 그 스피커들은 잘 작동한다.

→ The machine _______.

4 My dad drinks tea after breakfast. 나의 아빠는 아침 식사 후에 차를 마신다.

→ They _______.

5 We run really slowly. 우리는 정말 천천히 달린다.

→ Lauren _______.

6 Jason eats pizza on Saturdays. Jason은 토요일마다 피자를 먹는다.

→ We _______.

7 They stay home at night. 그들은 밤에 집에 있다.

→ He _______.

8 My brother plays soccer every weekend. 내 남동생은 주말마다 축구를 한다.

→ Ben and Ella _______.

9 Kelly spends too much money. Kelly는 돈을 너무 많이 쓴다.

→ You _______.

10 My trainers shout a lot. 내 트레이너들은 소리를 많이 지른다.

→ My coach _______.

B 밑줄 친 부분을 바르게 고쳐 문장을 다시 쓰세요.

1 Dora <u>speak</u> Spanish.　Dora는 스페인어를 한다.

→ _Dora speaks Spanish._

2 We <u>wants</u> a bowl of salad.　우리는 샐러드 한 그릇을 원한다.

→ ____

3 I <u>borrows</u> books from the library.　나는 도서관에서 책들을 빌린다.

→ ____

4 This hamburger <u>taste</u> really good.　이 햄버거는 정말 맛있다.

→ ____

5 It <u>look</u> like an interesting video.　그것은 흥미로운 영상처럼 보인다.

→ ____

6 I <u>cleans</u> the bathroom on Wednesdays.　나는 수요일마다 화장실을 청소한다.

→ ____

7 Bella and Larry <u>works</u> at the school.　Bella와 Larry는 학교에서 일한다.

→ ____

8 The loud sound <u>come</u> from there.　그 큰 소리는 저곳에서 나온다.

→ ____

9 The woman <u>sing</u> a song every night.　그 여자는 매일 밤 노래를 부른다.

→ ____

10 Pandas <u>eats</u> bamboo.　판다들은 대나무를 먹는다.

→ ____

A 우리말과 같은 뜻이 되도록 빈칸에 알맞은 말을 쓰세요.

1

Carl ________buys________ his clothes at the ________mall________ .

Carl은 그의 옷을 쇼핑몰에서 산다.

2

________________ ________________

________________ beautifully.

저 댄서들은 아름답게 춤춘다.

3

________________ ________________ from clouds.

눈은 구름으로부터 온다.

4

________________ ________________ Andy on

________________ .

그녀는 화요일마다 Andy를 만난다.

5

________________ ________________ a

________________ in the park.

나는 공원에서 자전거를 탄다.

6

________________ ________________

________________ on Sundays.

그들은 일요일마다 하키를 한다.

B 우리말과 같은 뜻이 되도록 빈칸에 알맞은 말을 쓰세요.

1 I ____________ some ____________ butter ____________ .
나는 약간의 버터를 원한다.

2 Roy ____________ ____________ ____________ .
Roy는 수영을 매우 잘한다.

3 Hanna ____________ ____________ .
Hanna는 커피를 싫어한다.

4 ____________ ____________ too much ____________ .
너는 너무 많은 물을 쓴다.

5 This mirror ____________ so ____________ .
이 거울은 아주 더러워 보인다.

6 ____________ ____________ a piece of ____________ .
그녀는 종이 한 장이 필요하다.

7 My dad ____________ ____________ ____________ breakfast.
나의 아빠는 아침 식사 후에 차를 마신다.

8 This ____________ ____________ so ____________ .
이 나무는 아주 빠르게 자란다.

9 ____________ ____________ ____________ every morning.
제빵사들은 매일 아침 빵을 굽는다.

10 Harry ____________ ____________ ____________ .
Harry는 로봇들을 가지고 논다.

11 Firefighters ____________ ____________ ____________ .
소방관들은 많은 생명을 구한다.

12 She ____________ the ____________ ____________ .
그녀는 혼자서 바닥을 청소한다.

일반동사의 3인칭 단수형 (1)

● 주어가 3인칭 단수일 때는 일반동사의 형태가 달라져요.

Stars **shine** brightly.
별들은 밝게 빛난다.

The sun **shines** brightly.
해는 밝게 빛난다.

● 대부분의 동사는 동사원형 끝에 **-s**를 붙여서 동사의 3인칭 단수형을 나타내요.

I / We / You / They 복수명사	동사원형	
He / She / It 단수명사 / 셀 수 없는 명사	동사원형 + **s**	~.

come 오다 → come**s**	sit 앉다 → sit**s**	read 읽다 → read**s**
like 좋아하다 → like**s**	speak 말하다 → speak**s**	drink 마시다 → drink**s**
want 원하다 → want**s**	play 놀다 → play**s**	open 열다 → open**s**

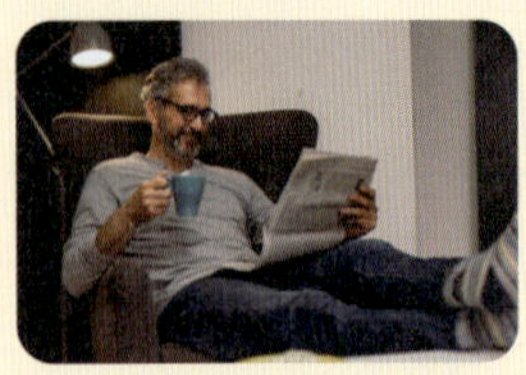

I drink a cup of tea at night.
나는 밤에 차 한 잔을 마신다.

→ He drink**s** a cup of tea at night.
그는 밤에 차 한 잔을 마신다.

They sit next to Jenna.
그들은 Jenna 옆에 앉는다.

→ Chris sit**s** next to Jenna.
Chris는 Jenna 옆에 앉는다.

CHECK UP

정답 및 해설 p.3

A 다음 주어에 알맞은 동사를 바르게 연결하세요.

1 I •

2 She •

3 His sister •

4 They •

5 The students •

6 Jeremy •

• ⓐ want some water.

• ⓑ wants some water.

B (   ) 안에서 알맞은 것을 고르세요.

1

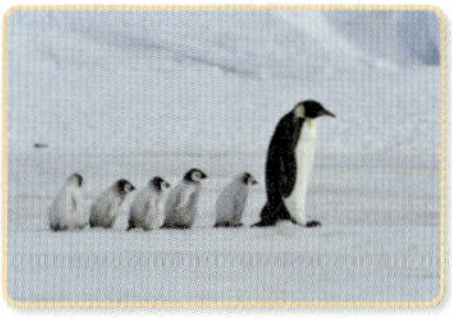

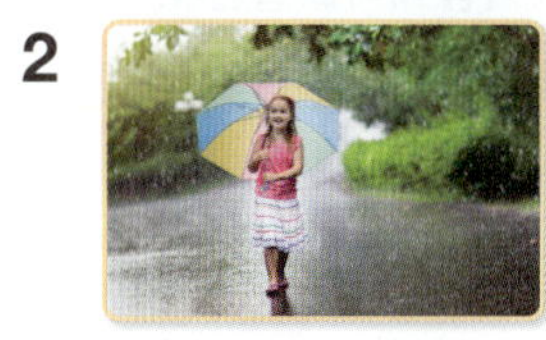

Penguins (walk / walks) very fast.

펭귄들은 매우 빠르게 걷는다.

2

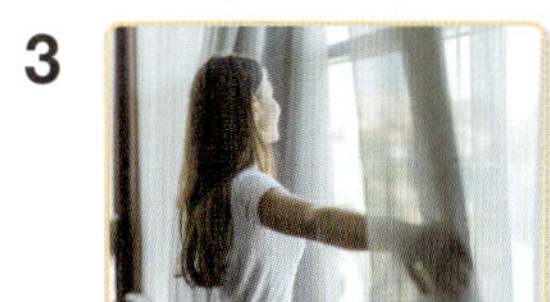

It (rain / rains) a lot in summer.

여름에 비가 많이 온다.

3

I (open / opens) the window at 9:00 a.m.

나는 오전 9시에 창문을 연다.

4

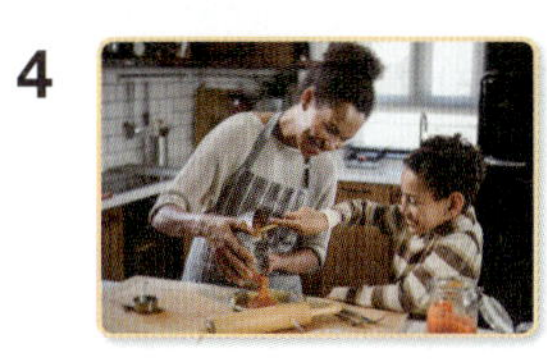

Eric (help / helps) his mom.

Eric은 그의 엄마를 돕는다.

일반동사의 3인칭 단수형 (2)

● 3인칭 단수형에 -s가 아니라 -es가 붙는 일반동사들도 있어요.

-s, -x, -ch, -sh, '자음 + o'로 끝나는 동사	동사원형 + **es**	pass 건네주다 → pass**es** touch 만지다 → touch**es** go 가다 → go**es**	fix 고치다 → fix**es** wash 씻다 → wash**es** do 하다 → do**es**

She fix**es** cars at work. 그녀는 일터에서 차들을 고친다.

It touch**es** my shoulder. 그것은 내 어깨에 닿는다.

Sam go**es** to the mall. Sam은 쇼핑몰에 간다.

● 동사가 '자음 + y'로 끝나는 경우에는 y를 i로 바꾸고 -es를 붙여요.

'자음 + **y**'로 끝나는 동사	-y → -ies	study 공부하다 → stud**ies** dry 말리다 → dr**ies** cry 울다 → cr**ies**	try 노력하다 → tr**ies** fly 날다 → fl**ies**

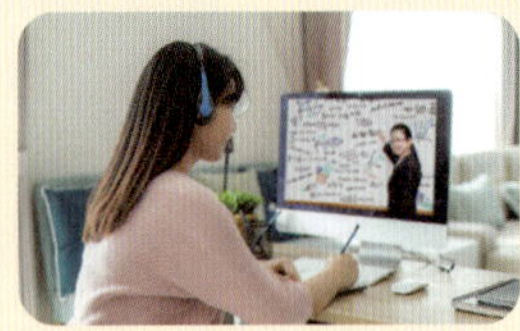

Kelly stud**ies** very hard. Kelly는 매우 열심히 공부한다.

He dr**ies** his hair every morning. 그는 매일 아침 머리를 말린다.

The bird fl**ies** high. 새는 높이 난다.

● 동사 have(가지다)의 3인칭 단수형은 위의 규칙을 따르지 않고 has로 써요.

She **has** a watch. 그녀는 시계를 가지고 있다.

The cat **has** a fat tail. 그 고양이는 통통한 꼬리를 가지고 있다.

정답 및 해설 p.3

A 다음 동사의 3인칭 단수형으로 알맞은 것을 고르세요.

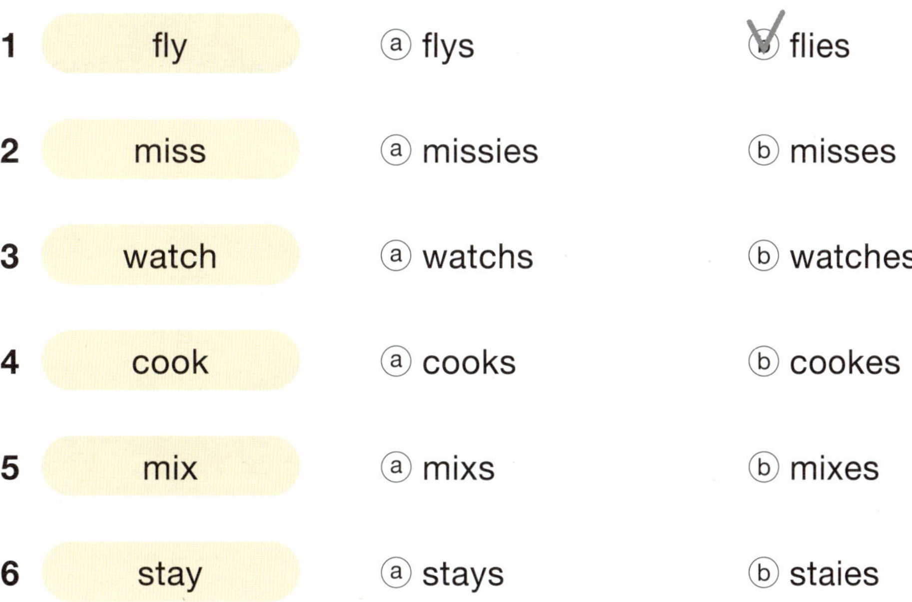

1 fly ⓐ flys ⓑ flies ✓

2 miss ⓐ missies ⓑ misses

3 watch ⓐ watchs ⓑ watches

4 cook ⓐ cooks ⓑ cookes

5 mix ⓐ mixs ⓑ mixes

6 stay ⓐ stays ⓑ staies

B ( ) 안에서 알맞은 것을 고르세요.

1 Mia (haves / (has)) a fever.   Mia는 열이 있다.

2 She (drives / drivees) so fast.   그녀는 매우 빠르게 운전한다.

3 He (studys / studies) Spanish after school.   그는 방과 후에 스페인어를 공부한다.

4 He (dos / does) yoga in the evening.   그는 저녁에 요가를 한다.

5 It (snows / snowes) a lot in winter.   겨울에는 눈이 많이 온다.

6 Her cat (scratchs / scratches) the wall.   그녀의 고양이는 벽을 긁는다.

−s가 붙는 일반동사의
3인칭 단수형을 알아봐요.

A 보기의 빈칸에 들어갈 수 있는 동사에 ○ 표시하세요.

1 보기 She ________ her dog.

(loves)	walk
trains	hates
feed	like

2 보기 They ________ very well.

swim	sleep
cooks	sing
acts	dance

B 밑줄 친 부분을 바르게 고쳐 쓰세요.

1 I <u>wants</u> a new laptop.　　　　　➡　____want____
나는 새 노트북 컴퓨터를 원한다.

2 She <u>read</u> the novel every day.　　➡　__________
그녀는 매일 그 소설을 읽는다.

3 We <u>feels</u> happy.　　　　　　　　➡　__________
우리는 행복하다고 느낀다.

4 This candy <u>taste</u> like watermelon.　➡　__________
이 사탕은 수박 맛이 난다.

5 Lilly and Ben <u>takes</u> photos together.　➡　__________
Lilly와 Ben은 함께 사진들을 찍는다.

6 My dad <u>need</u> some sugar.　　　　➡　__________
나의 아빠는 약간의 설탕이 필요하다.

LET'S PRACTICE 2

-es, -ies가 붙는 일반동사의 3인칭 단수형을 알아봐요.

A 다음 동사의 3인칭 단수형을 쓰세요.

1 go → *goes*

2 catch → __________

3 cry → __________

4 open → __________

5 brush → __________

6 say → __________

7 relax → __________

B 밑줄 친 부분이 맞으면 ◯, 틀리면 X 표시하세요.

1 She <u>carries</u> a big backpack.   그녀는 커다란 배낭을 가지고 다닌다.   ◯

2 He <u>fixs</u> the curtain in the bedroom.   그는 침실에 있는 커튼을 고친다.   

3 Nate <u>loves</u> pop music.   Nate는 팝 음악을 매우 좋아한다.   

4 The kangaroo <u>jumpes</u> really high.   저 캥거루는 매우 높게 점프한다.   

5 My uncle <u>enjoys</u> skiing.   내 삼촌은 스키 타는 것을 즐긴다.   

6 Sophia <u>dryes</u> her hair in the bathroom.   
Sophia는 그녀의 머리를 화장실에서 말린다.

A 보기 에서 알맞은 단어를 골라 쓰세요.

> 보기   teaches   washes   plays   remember   flies   has
>
>   speaks   look   live   grows   goes

1 My uncle ______teaches______ math.   내 삼촌은 수학을 가르친다.

2 Chris ______________ Korean.   Chris는 한국어를 한다.

3 This plant ______________ in warm weather.   이 식물은 따뜻한 날씨에서 자란다.

4 They ______________ in a big city.   그들은 대도시에 산다.

5 She ______________ to the gym every day.   그녀는 매일 체육관에 간다.

6 Olivia ______________ four dresses.   Olivia는 드레스를 네 벌 가지고 있다.

7 I ______________ my grandmother.   나는 내 할머니를 기억한다.

8 Meg ______________ her hands with soap.   Meg는 그녀의 손을 비누로 씻는다.

9 The bird ______________ quickly.   그 새는 빠르게 난다.

10 You ______________ cold.   너는 추워 보인다.

11 Stella ______________ baseball after school.   Stella는 방과 후에 야구를 한다.

B 주어진 동사를 알맞은 현재형으로 바꿔 문장을 완성하세요.

1 Lisa ___________misses___________ her hometown. (miss)
Lisa는 그녀의 고향을 그리워한다.

2 He _________________ some bread for lunch. (eat)
그는 점심으로 빵을 조금 먹는다.

3 We _________________ that movie. (know)
우리는 저 영화를 안다.

4 The man _________________ heavy boxes every day. (carry)
그 남자는 매일 무거운 상자들을 옮긴다.

5 Jeremy _________________ after you. (come)
Jeremy는 네 뒤에 온다.

6 The curtain _________________ the floor. (touch)
커튼이 바닥에 닿는다.

7 I _________________ yellow sneakers. (want)
나는 노란색 운동화를 원한다.

8 My mom _________________ my photos. (like)
우리 엄마는 내 사진들을 좋아한다.

9 My daughter _________________ a spoon and a fork. (use)
내 딸은 숟가락과 포크를 사용한다.

10 Engineers _________________ old machines. (fix)
엔지니어들은 오래된 기계들을 고친다.

A 사진을 보고 주어진 말을 이용하여 빈칸에 알맞은 말을 쓰세요.

1 

The bridge ___crosses___ the river. (cross)
그 다리는 강을 가로지른다.

2 

The candy _____________ like lemon. (taste)
그 사탕은 레몬 맛이 난다.

3 

We _____________ to school. (walk)
우리는 학교에 걸어간다.

4 

She _____________ a kite on weekends. (fly)
그녀는 주말마다 연을 날린다.

5 

The swans _____________ in the lake. (swim)
백조들이 호수에서 헤엄을 친다.

6 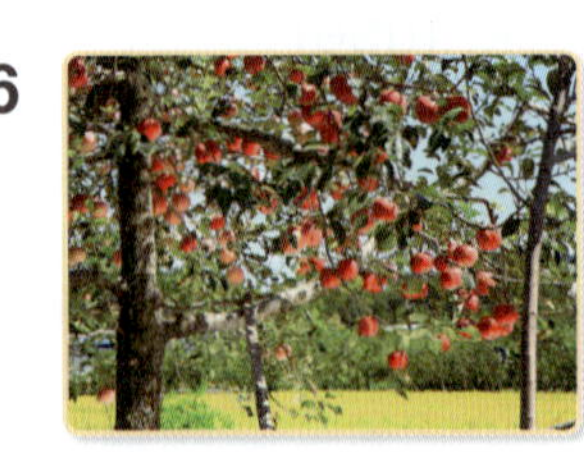

Dan _____________ some apple trees in his garden. (have)
Dan은 그의 정원에 몇 그루의 사과 나무를 가지고 있다.

B 우리말과 같은 뜻이 되도록 보기 에서 알맞은 단어를 골라 쓰세요. (필요하면 형태를 바꾸세요.)

| 보기 | try | live | forget | jump | drive | finish |
| | have | rain | shine | teach | study | |

1 They ______live______ in a small town.   그들은 작은 마을에 산다.

2 I ______________ a tablet PC.   나는 태블릿 PC를 가지고 있다.

3 Her smile ______________ brightly.   그녀의 미소는 밝게 빛난다.

4 He ______________ American history.   그는 미국 역사를 공부한다.

5 She ______________ to the airport.   그녀는 공항에 운전해서 간다.

6 The boy ______________ to be healthy.   그 소년은 건강해지려고 노력한다.

7 Gina often ______________ their names.   Gina는 자주 그들의 이름을 잊는다.

8 It ______________ a lot in June.   6월에는 비가 많이 온다.

9 The play ______________ at 9:00 p.m.   그 연극은 오후 9시에 끝난다.

10 He ______________ science in middle school.   그는 중학교에서 과학을 가르친다.

11 The puppy ______________ really high.   그 강아지는 아주 높게 점프한다.

A 주어진 동사를 빈칸에 알맞은 현재형으로 쓰세요.

1 I _______pay_______ two dollars every week. (pay)   나는 매주 2달러를 지불한다.

Ann _______pays_______ three dollars every month.   Ann은 매달 3달러를 지불한다.

2 His pictures _______________ my eye. (catch)   그의 그림들은 내 눈길을 잡는다.

The early bird _______________ the worm.   일찍 일어나는 새가 벌레를 잡는다.

3 He _______________ sad. (feel)   그는 슬프다고 느낀다.

They _______________ lonely.   그들은 외롭다고 느낀다.

4 She _______________ her homework at night. (do)   그녀는 밤에 숙제를 한다.

Dan and Kate _______________ their work at night.   Dan과 Kate는 밤에 일을 한다.

5 They _______________ to win the game (try).   그들은 경기에서 이기려고 노력한다.

My cat _______________ to touch the button.   내 고양이는 버튼을 건드리려고 노력한다.

6 My son _______________ the two colors. (mix)   내 아들은 두 가지의 색을 섞는다.

They _______________ salt and flour.   그들은 소금과 밀가루를 섞는다.

7 It _______________ some time. (save)   그것은 약간의 시간을 절약해 준다.

You _______________ your money in a piggy bank.   너는 네 돈을 돼지 저금통에 저축한다.

8 We _______________ our teeth every day. (brush)   우리는 매일 이를 닦는다.

He _______________ his hair in the morning.   그는 아침에 머리를 빗는다.

B 다음 문장을 주어진 주어로 시작하는 문장으로 바꿔 쓰세요.

1 I cross the road. 나는 길을 건넌다.

➜ She _________ crosses the road _________.

2 Heidi lives in New York. Heidi는 뉴욕에 산다.

➜ Heidi and Alex _________.

3 My parents try to be helpful. 내 부모님은 도움이 되기 위해 노력하신다.

➜ My mom _________.

4 His hands touch the shelf. 그의 손은 선반에 닿는다.

➜ His head _________.

5 My brother passes the ball very well. 내 남동생은 공을 매우 잘 패스한다.

➜ We _________.

6 We go to the market by bus. 우리는 시장에 버스를 타고 간다.

➜ He _________.

7 A dog follows you. 개 한 마리가 너를 따라온다.

➜ Two cats _________.

8 Terry grows some tomatoes. Terry는 토마토를 조금 키운다.

➜ My classmates _________.

9 I have a stomachache. 나는 복통이 있다.

➜ Sarah _________.

10 He fixes the roof. 그는 지붕을 고친다.

➜ They _________.

STEP UP 4

A 밑줄 친 부분을 바르게 고쳐 문장을 다시 쓰세요.

1 She <u>haves</u> two belts.   그녀는 두 개의 벨트를 가지고 있다.
→ _______________ She has two belts. _______________

2 We <u>studies</u> Chinese history.   우리는 중국 역사를 공부한다.
→ ____

3 Daniel <u>remember</u> his aunt.   Daniel은 그의 이모를 기억한다.
→ ____

4 My baby <u>crys</u> a lot.   내 아기는 많이 운다.
→ ____

5 My father <u>actes</u> on the stage.   내 아버지는 무대에서 연기하신다.
→ ____

6 They <u>washes</u> their feet in the bathroom.   그들은 욕실에서 발을 씻는다.
→ ____

7 I <u>uses</u> chopsticks very well.   나는 젓가락을 아주 잘 사용한다.
→ ____

8 The machine <u>make</u> a lot of noise.   그 기계는 많은 소음을 낸다.
→ ____

9 I <u>misses</u> the cafeteria in my hometown.   나는 내 고향에 있는 그 식당이 그립다.
→ ____

10 Bears <u>sleeps</u> in the winter.   곰들은 겨울에 잠을 잔다.
→ ____

B 우리말과 같은 뜻이 되도록 주어진 말을 이용하여 문장을 완성하세요.

1 지수는 매일 아침 스페인어를 공부한다. (study Spanish)

➡ Jisu _______studies Spanish_______ every morning.

2 그는 아침에 주스 한 잔을 마신다. (drink a glass of juice)

➡ He __________________________ in the morning.

3 나의 새 신발은 밝게 빛난다. (shine brightly)

➡ My new shoes __________________________.

4 Anna는 쇼핑몰까지 운전해서 간다. (drive to the mall)

➡ Anna __________________________.

5 내 여동생은 매일 빵집에 간다. (go to the bakery)

➡ My sister __________________________ every day.

6 너는 패스트푸드를 너무 많이 먹는다. (eat too much fast food)

➡ You __________________________.

7 그 콘서트는 11시에 끝난다. (finish at 11 o'clock)

➡ The concert __________________________.

8 Joe는 내 옆에 앉는다. (sit next to me)

➡ Joe __________________________.

9 그 접착제는 매우 빨리 마른다. (dry so fast)

➡ The glue __________________________.

A 우리말과 같은 뜻이 되도록 빈칸에 알맞은 말을 쓰세요.

1

You _______look_______ _______cold_______.
너는 추워 보인다.

2

______________ ______________ ______________ so fast.
그 접착제는 매우 빨리 마른다.

3

Her ______________ ______________ the ______________.
그녀의 고양이는 벽을 긁는다.

4

Meg ______________ ______________ ______________ with soap.
Meg는 그녀의 손을 비누로 씻는다.

5

My daughter ______________ a ______________ and a ______________.
내 딸은 숟가락과 포크를 사용한다.

6

______________ ______________ ______________ on the ______________.
내 아버지는 무대에서 연기하신다.

B 우리말과 같은 뜻이 되도록 빈칸에 알맞은 말을 쓰세요.

1 Sam ______goes______ ______to______ the ______mall______.

Sam은 쇼핑몰에 간다.

2 We ______________ ______________ ______________.

우리는 학교에 걸어간다.

3 He ______________ ______________ in the evening.

그는 저녁에 요가를 한다.

4 She ______________ ______________ at ______________.

그녀는 일터에서 차들을 고친다.

5 This candy ______________ ______________ ______________.

이 사탕은 수박 맛이 난다.

6 ______________ ______________ ______________ ______________ in summer.

여름에 비가 많이 온다.

7 Lilly and Ben ______________ ______________ ______________.

Lilly와 Ben은 함께 사진들을 찍는다.

8 My ______________ ______________.

내 삼촌은 수학을 가르친다.

9 We ______________ ______________ ______________.

우리는 저 영화를 안다.

10 I ______________ ______________ ______________.

나는 노란색 운동화를 원한다.

11 Sophia ______________ ______________ ______________ in the bathroom.

Sophia는 그녀의 머리를 화장실에서 말린다.

12 Lisa ______________ ______________ ______________.

Lisa는 그녀의 고향을 그리워한다.

[1~3] 사진을 보고 보기 에서 알맞은 단어를 골라 쓰세요. (필요하면 형태를 바꾸세요.)

보기	look　　　run　　　drink

1 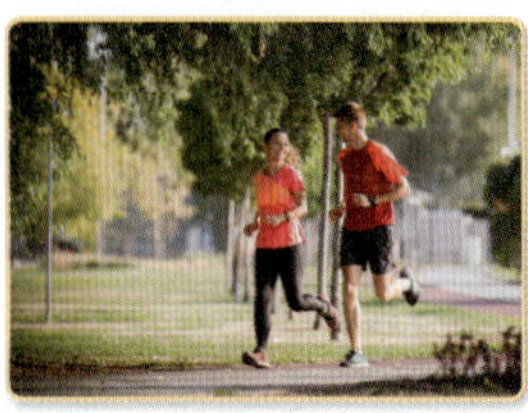

They _____________ in the park every morning.

2 

He _____________ milk every day.

3 

The kitchen _____________ clean.

4 일반동사가 <u>아닌</u> 것을 고르세요.

① buy　　　　② have　　　　③ is　　　　④ come

5 동사원형과 3인칭 단수형이 <u>잘못</u> 짝지어진 것을 고르세요.

① dry – drys　　　　② sit – sits
③ go – goes　　　　④ have – has

6 빈칸에 들어갈 알맞은 말을 고르세요.

> Patrick ______________ to work by bus every day.

① is   ② are   ③ go   ④ goes

7 빈칸에 들어갈 수 <u>없는</u> 말을 고르세요.

> ______________ plays golf on Sundays.

① James   ② They   ③ My aunt   ④ He

[8~9] 밑줄 친 부분이 <u>어색한</u> 것을 고르세요.

8 ① Nate <u>buys</u> books online.

② You <u>speaks</u> Spanish very well.

③ The museum <u>closes</u> on Mondays.

④ I <u>drink</u> two cups of coffee every day.

9 ① Bill and I <u>ride</u> bicycles on Saturdays.

② We <u>wear</u> school uniforms.

③ The class <u>begin</u> at 10:00 a.m.

④ Julia <u>walks</u> to school every morning.

[10~11] 빈칸에 들어갈 말이 바르게 짝지어진 것을 고르세요.

10

· Ms. Jackson ______________ movies.
· Rabbits ______________ carrots.

① enjoys – like
② enjoys – likes
③ enjoies – like
④ enjoies – likes

11

· Matt and Katie ______________ at the hospital.
· A spider ______________ eight legs.

① work – haves
② works – haves
③ work – has
④ works – has

12 어법상 <u>틀린</u> 문장을 고르세요.

① The candy tastes salty.
② I often wash my hands.
③ The kids like toys.
④ My sister go jogging every morning.

13 우리말과 같은 뜻이 되도록 빈칸에 알맞은 말을 쓰세요.

내 사촌은 베이징에 산다.

My cousin ______________ in Beijing.

14 우리말과 같은 뜻이 되도록 주어진 말을 이용하여 문장을 완성하세요.

그녀는 중학교에서 일본어를 가르친다. (teach, Japanese)

→ ______________________________________ in a middle school.

15 다음 Jane의 일과표를 보고 빈칸에 알맞은 말을 쓰세요.

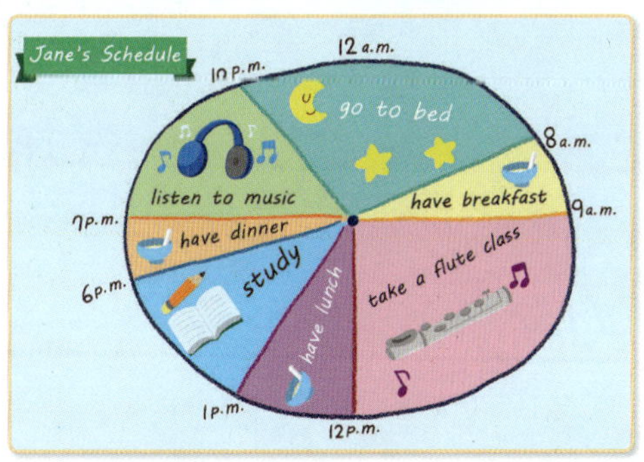

Jane ____________ breakfast at 8:00 a.m. She ____________
a flute class in the morning. She ____________ in the
afternoon. After dinner, she ____________ to music. She
____________ to bed at 10:00 p.m.

Chapter 02

일반동사의 부정문과 의문문

Unit 01 일반동사의 부정문

Unit 02 일반동사의 의문문

학습목표

1 일반동사의 부정문을 만드는 법을 알아보아요.
2 일반동사의 의문문을 만드는 법을 알아보아요.
3 일반동사의 의문문에 대답하는 법을 알아보아요.

모르는 단어에 체크해 보세요.

frog
개구리

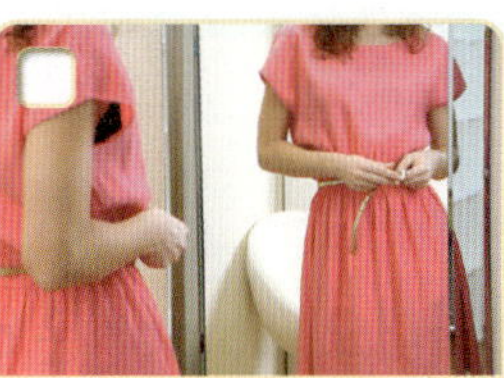
fit
꼭 맞다

football
풋볼

climb
오르다

bark
짖다

address
주소

goat
염소

giraffe
기린

freeze
얼다

fight
싸우다

cabbage
양배추

bookstore
서점

witch
마녀

letter
편지

answer
정답

horrible
무서운

leave
떠나다

skate
스케이트를 타다

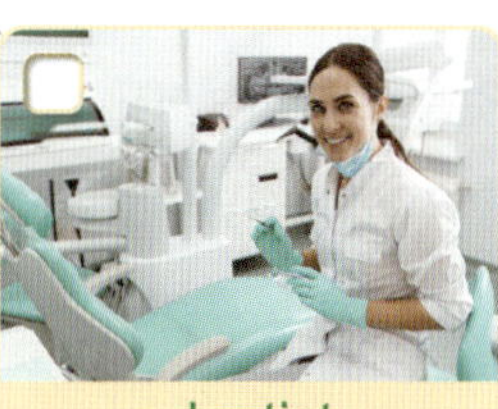
dentist
치과 의사

jogging
조깅

Unit 01

일반동사의 부정문

● 일반동사의 부정문은 동사 앞에 do not을 써서 나타내요. do not 은 don't로 줄여 쓸 수 있어요.

I / You / We / They 복수명사	**do not** **(= don't)**	동사원형 ~.

I **like** milk. 나는 우유를 좋아한다.
I **do not** like milk. 나는 우유를 좋아하지 않는다.

We **don't** speak Japanese. 우리는 일본어를 하지 않는다.
They **don't** read comic books. 그들은 만화책을 읽지 않는다.
Those frogs **don't** look healthy. 저 개구리들은 건강해 보이지 않는다.

● 주어가 3인칭 단수일 때는 does not을 써요. does not은 doesn't로 줄여 쓸 수 있어요.

He / She / It 단수명사 / 셀 수 없는 명사	**does not** **(= doesn't)**	동사원형 ~.

He **listens** to his mother. 그는 그의 엄마의 말을 듣는다.
He **does not** listen to his mother. 그는 그의 엄마의 말을 듣지 않는다.

It **doesn't** look fun. 그것은 재미있어 보이지 않는다.
This T-shirt **doesn't** fit my body. 이 티셔츠는 내 몸에 맞지 않는다.
She **doesn't** use David's pen. 그녀는 David의 펜을 사용하지 않는다.

> **Tip** does not 뒤에 오는 동사에는 -(e)s가 붙지 않아요.
> She **does not** wear a jacket. (O) 그녀는 재킷을 입지 않는다.
> She **does not** wears a jacket. (X)

CHECK UP

정답 및 해설 p.4

A 일반동사의 부정문에 V 표시하세요.

1 I do not eat carrots.   나는 당근을 먹지 않는다. 

2 He does not run here.   그는 여기에서 뛰지 않는다.

3 It isn't rainy today.   오늘은 비가 오지 않는다.

4 We don't know each other.   우리는 서로 모른다.

5 They do their homework together.   그들은 함께 숙제를 한다.

6 Jessica doesn't trust Emma.   Jessica는 Emma를 신뢰하지 않는다.

7 You don't tell the truth.   너는 진실을 말하지 않는다.

B 밑줄 친 부분이 맞으면 ○, 틀리면 X 표시하세요.

1 I <u>don't hurt</u> you.   나는 너를 아프게 하지 않는다. 

2 Cathy <u>do not cook</u> tonight.   Cathy는 오늘 밤 요리하지 않는다.

3 The story <u>doesn't sounds</u> scary.   그 이야기는 무섭게 들리지 않는다.

4 They <u>doesn't have</u> a test today.   그들은 오늘 시험을 보지 않는다.

5 Koalas <u>don't eat</u> fish.   코알라들은 생선을 먹지 않는다.

6 She <u>doesn't tell</u> lies.   그녀는 거짓말을 하지 않는다.

일반동사의 의문문

● 일반동사의 의문문은 「Do[Does] + 주어 + 동사원형 ~?」으로 나타내요.

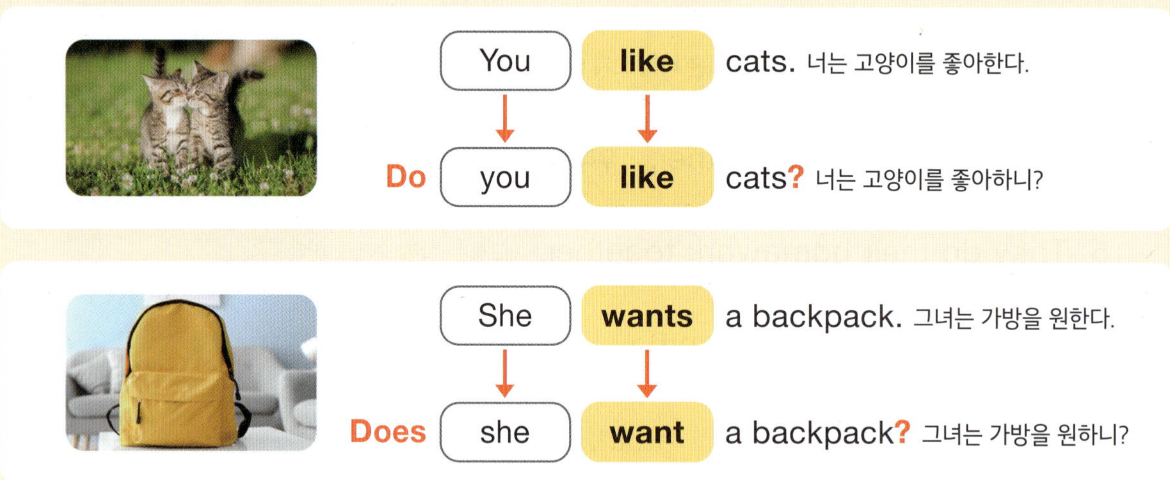

● 의문문에 대한 긍정 대답은 「Yes, 주어 + do[does].」, 부정 대답은 「No, 주어 + don't[doesn't].」로 나타내요.

Do you **know** Jamie? 너는 Jamie를 아니?
Yes, I **do**. / **No**, I **don't**.
응, 그래.　　　아니, 그렇지 않아.

Does Dana **sleep** on the sofa? Dana는 소파에서 자니?
Yes, she **does**. / **No**, she **doesn't**.
응, 그래.　　　　　아니, 그렇지 않아.

> **Tip** 의문문의 주어가 일반명사일 때는 주어를 대명사로 바꿔서 대답해요.
>
> Does **your sister** swim in the pool? 너의 여동생은 수영장에서 수영하니?
>
> Yes, **she** does. 응, 그래. / No, **she** doesn't. 아니, 그렇지 않아.

A 빈칸에 들어갈 말로 알맞은 것을 고르세요.

1 __________ you love your brother?   ✓ⓐ Do   ⓑ Does
너는 너의 오빠를 사랑하니?

2 __________ she drink coffee?   ⓐ Do   ⓑ Does
그녀는 커피를 마시니?

3 __________ Ellen need some paper?   ⓐ Do   ⓑ Does
Ellen은 종이가 조금 필요하니?

4 __________ they play football after school?   ⓐ Do   ⓑ Does
그들은 방과 후에 풋볼을 하니?

5 __________ monkeys climb trees?   ⓐ Do   ⓑ Does
원숭이들은 나무를 오르니?

B (   ) 안에서 알맞은 것을 고르세요.

1 A: Does she play the guitar?   그녀는 기타를 연주하니?
B: (Yes / No), she doesn't.   아니, 그렇지 않아.

2 A: (Do / Does) they cook dinner?   그들은 저녁을 요리하니?
B: Yes, they do.   응, 그래.

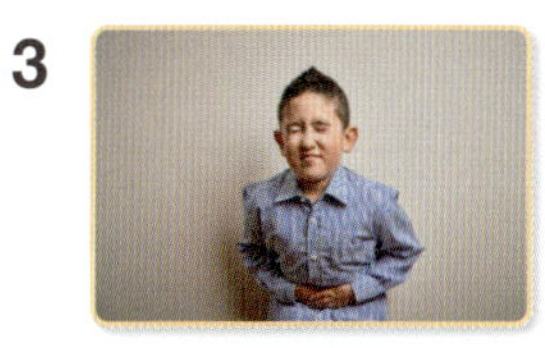

3 A: Does your head hurt?   너의 머리가 아프니?
B: No, it (does / doesn't).   아니, 그렇지 않아.

4 A: (Do / Does) we need a tent?   우리는 텐트가 필요하니?
B: Yes, we (do / does).   응, 그래.

일반동사의 부정문 형태를
익혀요.

A ( ) 안에서 알맞은 것을 고르세요.

1 They (**don't** / doesn't) like horror movies.
그들은 무서운 영화를 좋아하지 않는다.

2 He (don't / doesn't) miss his old house.
그는 그의 옛 집을 그리워하지 않는다.

3 Bell (don't / doesn't) have black hair.
Bell은 검은 머리를 가지고 있지 않다.

4 Irene doesn't (exercise / exercises) every day.
Irene은 매일 운동하지 않는다.

5 My dogs don't (bark / barks) at all.
내 개들은 전혀 짖지 않는다.

B 밑줄 친 부분을 바르게 고쳐 쓰세요.

1 Rabbits <u>doesn't</u> climb trees. ➡ ___don't[do not]___
토끼들은 나무를 오르지 않는다.

2 She doesn't <u>works</u> at the school. ➡ __________
그녀는 그 학교에서 일하지 않는다.

3 The apple juice <u>do not</u> taste bitter. ➡ __________
그 사과 주스는 쓴 맛이 나지 않는다.

4 The show <u>don't</u> start at 4:00 p.m. ➡ __________
그 쇼는 오후 4시에 시작하지 않는다.

5 Those dancers don't <u>jumps</u> high. ➡ __________
저 무용수들은 높이 점프하지 않는다.

6 They <u>doesn't</u> need any money. ➡ __________
그들은 어떤 돈도 필요하지 않다.

LET'S PRACTICE 2

일반동사의 의문문과 그에 대한 대답을 연습해요.

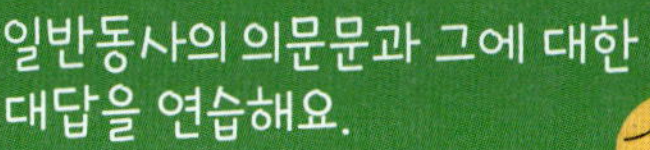

A 빈칸에 Do 또는 Does 중 알맞은 것을 쓰세요.

1 _____Do_____ you know my address?　너는 내 주소를 알고 있니?

2 ___________ it start at 8:00 a.m.?　그것은 오전 8시에 시작하니?

3 ___________ they raise goats?　그들은 염소들을 키우니?

4 ___________ his fans feel happy?　그의 팬들은 행복하다고 느끼니?

5 ___________ his teacher smile?　그의 선생님은 미소를 짓니?

6 ___________ Jake go to school today?　Jake는 오늘 학교에 가니?

7 ___________ I look like a liar?　나는 거짓말쟁이처럼 보이니?

B 보기 에서 알맞은 말을 골라 쓰세요.

보기	do	does	don't	doesn't

1 A: Does the earth go around the sun?　지구는 태양 주위를 도니?

　B: Yes, it _____does_____.　응, 그래.

2 A: Do you watch TV at night?　너는 밤에 TV를 보니?

　B: No, I ___________.　아니, 그렇지 않아.

3 A: Do giraffes eat leaves?　기린들은 나뭇잎들을 먹니?

　B: Yes, they ___________.　응, 그래.

4 A: Does water freeze at 100℃?　물은 섭씨 100도에서 어니?

　B: No, it ___________.　아니, 그렇지 않아.

A 빈칸에 알맞은 말을 써서 부정문으로 바꾸세요. (축약형으로 쓰세요.)

1 The monster has a big mouth.   그 괴물은 큰 입을 가지고 있다.

→ The monster ____doesn't____ ____have____ a big mouth.

2 They like chocolate cake.   그들은 초콜릿 케이크를 좋아한다.

→ They ____________ ____________ chocolate cake.

3 He wears glasses.   그는 안경을 쓴다.

→ He ____________ ____________ glasses.

4 My grandmother enjoys classical music.   내 할머니는 클래식 음악을 즐기신다.

→ My grandmother ____________ ____________ classical music.

5 We use the telephone on the table.   우리는 테이블 위의 전화기를 쓴다.

→ We ____________ ____________ the telephone on the table.

6 Stella remembers all of you.   Stella는 너희 모두를 기억한다.

→ Stella ____________ ____________ all of you.

7 The bakery closes at 9:00 p.m.   그 빵집은 오후 9시에 닫는다.

→ The bakery ____________ ____________ at 9:00 p.m.

8 My classmates study very hard.   내 반 친구들은 매우 열심히 공부한다.

→ My classmates ____________ ____________ very hard.

9 She understands John's ideas.   그녀는 John의 생각들을 이해한다.

→ She ____________ ____________ John's ideas.

10 I miss my old friends.   나는 내 옛 친구들이 그립다.

→ I ____________ ____________ my old friends.

B 빈칸에 알맞은 말을 써서 의문문으로 바꾸세요.

1 She lives in Canada. 그녀는 캐나다에 산다.

→ _____Does_____ _____she_____ live in Canada?

2 Snakes sleep all winter. 뱀들은 겨울 내내 잔다.

→ _____________ _____________ sleep all winter?

3 Nick gets up at 7:00 a.m. Nick은 오전 7시에 일어난다.

→ _____________ _____________ get up at 7:00 a.m.?

4 We need a small bowl. 우리는 작은 그릇이 필요하다.

→ _____________ _____________ need a small bowl?

C 빈칸에 알맞은 말을 넣어 대화를 완성하세요.

1 A: Do you ride your bike on Mondays? 너는 월요일마다 자전거를 타니?

　B: Yes, _____I_____ _____do_____ . 응, 그래.

2 A: Does she want some more milk? 그녀는 우유를 좀 더 원하니?

　B: No, _____________ _____________ . 아니, 그렇지 않아.

3 A: Do your parents have a car? 네 부모님은 차를 가지고 있으시니?

　B: No, _____________ _____________ . 아니, 그렇지 않아.

4 A: Does your brother play baseball? 네 남동생은 야구를 하니?

　B: Yes, _____________ _____________ . 응, 그래.

A 우리말과 같은 뜻이 되도록 주어진 말을 이용하여 문장을 완성하세요.

1 Emily와 Dan은 매일 싸우니? (fight)

➡ _____Do_____ Emily and Dan _____fight_____ every day?

2 나는 학교에 지하철을 타고 가지 않는다. (go)

➡ I ___________ ___________ to school by subway.

3 Tiffany는 이모가 없다. (have)

➡ Tiffany ___________ ___________ an aunt.

4 그는 아침에 늦게 일어나니? (get up)

➡ ___________ he ___________ ___________ late in the morning?

5 우리는 숟가락과 포크가 필요하니? (need)

➡ ___________ we ___________ spoons and forks?

6 내 친구는 흐린 날들을 좋아하지 않는다. (like)

➡ My friend ___________ ___________ cloudy days.

7 너의 아들은 양배추를 먹니? (eat)

➡ ___________ your son ___________ cabbage?

8 그들은 스페인어를 하지 않는다. (speak)

➡ They ___________ ___________ Spanish.

9 너는 그렇게 자주 노래하지 않는다. (sing)

➡ You ___________ ___________ very often.

10 그 서점은 잡지들을 파니? (sell)

➡ ___________ the bookstore ___________ magazines?

B 사진을 보고 주어진 말을 이용하여 빈칸에 알맞은 말을 쓰세요.

1

A: _____Does_____ Jake _____take_____ piano lessons these days? (take)   Jake는 요즘 피아노 수업을 듣니?

B: Yes, he _____does_____.   응, 그래.

2

Ron _____________ _____________ brown eyes. (have)   Ron은 갈색 눈을 가지고 있지 않다.

3

I _____________ _____________ vegetables. (want)

나는 채소를 원하지 않는다.

4

A: _____________ you _____________ in the pool? (swim)   너희는 수영장에서 수영을 하니?

B: _____________, we don't.   아니, 그렇지 않아.

5

A: _____________ he _____________ TV in the morning? (watch)   그는 아침에 TV를 보니?

B: _____________, he does.   응, 그래.

6

I _____________ _____________ good today. (feel)

나는 오늘 몸이 좋지 않다.

STEP UP 3

A 우리말과 같은 뜻이 되도록 보기 에서 알맞은 단어를 골라 부정문을 완성하세요.

보기
know　　sell　　play　　understand　　study
exercise　　tell　　read　　end　　use

1 The witch ___doesn't___ ___tell___ the truth.
그 마녀는 진실을 말하지 않는다.

2 He ______________ ______________ a book every night.
그는 매일 밤 책을 읽지 않는다.

3 I ______________ ______________ my mom's letter.
나는 엄마의 편지를 이해하지 못한다.

4 Her sister ______________ ______________ French.
그녀의 여동생은 프랑스어를 공부하지 않는다.

5 The movie ______________ ______________ at 5:00 p.m.
그 영화는 오후 5시에 끝나지 않는다.

6 We ______________ ______________ that knife anymore.
우리는 더 이상 저 칼을 사용하지 않는다.

7 They ______________ ______________ after work.
그들은 일이 끝난 후에 운동하지 않는다.

8 The store ______________ ______________ potatoes.
그 가게는 감자를 팔지 않는다.

9 Leo ______________ ______________ the harp.
Leo는 하프를 연주하지 않는다.

10 These men ______________ ______________ the answer.
이 남자들은 답을 알고 있지 않다.

B 주어진 말을 이용하여 대화를 완성하세요.

1 A: _____Does_____ it _____rain_____ a lot in summer? (rain) 여름에 비가 많이 오니?

B: Yes, _____it_____ _____does_____. 응, 그래.

2 A: ___________ her dogs ___________ carrots? (eat)
그녀의 강아지들은 당근을 먹니?

B: No, ___________ ___________. 아니, 그렇지 않아.

3 A: ___________ people ___________ happy here? (look)
사람들은 이곳에서 행복해 보이니?

B: No, ___________ ___________. 아니, 그렇지 않아.

4 A: ___________ Kate ___________ poor people? (help)
Kate는 불쌍한 사람들을 돕니?

B: Yes, ___________ ___________. 응, 그래.

5 A: ___________ he ___________ this week? (work) 그는 이번 주에 일하니?

B: No, ___________ ___________. 아니, 그렇지 않아.

6 A: ___________ the story ___________ horrible? (sound)
그 이야기는 무섭게 들리니?

B: Yes, ___________ ___________. 응, 그래.

7 A: ___________ Ian and Joe ___________ me? (hate)
Ian과 Joe는 나를 싫어하니?

B: No, ___________ ___________. 아니, 그렇지 않아.

8 A: ___________ the boy ___________ more time? (need)
그 소년은 시간이 더 필요하니?

B: Yes, ___________ ___________. 응, 그래.

A 다음 문장을 주어진 지시대로 바꿔 쓰세요. (부정문은 축약형으로 쓰세요.)

1 Bears sleep all winter. (의문문) 곰들은 겨울 내내 잔다.

→ _______________ Do bears sleep all winter? _______________

2 The train leaves at 4:30 a.m. (부정문) 그 기차는 오전 4시 30분에 떠난다.

→ _______________

3 This blanket feels soft. (의문문) 이 담요는 부드럽게 느껴진다.

→ _______________

4 I enjoy skating. (부정문) 나는 스케이트 타는 것을 즐긴다.

→ _______________

5 He likes sad movies. (부정문) 그는 슬픈 영화를 좋아한다.

→ _______________

6 Britney goes to bed early. (의문문) Britney는 일찍 잔다.

→ _______________

7 Those girls live in Kenya. (부정문) 저 소녀들은 케냐에 산다.

→ _______________

8 They go to the dentist. (의문문) 그들은 치과에 간다.

→ _______________

9 Annie dances very well. (부정문) Annie는 춤을 매우 잘 춘다.

→ _______________

10 My socks look clean. (의문문) 내 양말은 깨끗해 보인다.

→ _______________

B 다음 표를 보고 주어진 말을 이용하여 문장을 완성하세요.

	Monday	Tuesday	Wednesday
Mia	play tennis	go jogging	read books
James	play soccer	walk his dog	ride his bike

1 A: ______Does______ Mia ______play______ _____tennis_____ on Mondays?
Mia는 월요일마다 테니스를 치니?

B: Yes, ______she______ _____does_____. 응, 그래.

2 A: ____________ Mia play soccer on Tuesdays?
Mia는 화요일마다 축구를 하니?

B: ____________, ____________ ____________. 아니, 그렇지 않아.

3 A: ____________ Mia ____________ ____________ on Wednesdays?
Mia는 수요일마다 책을 읽니?

B: Yes, ____________ ____________. 응, 그래.

4 A: ____________ James ____________ ____________ on Mondays?
James는 월요일마다 조깅을 하러 가니?

B: No, ____________ ____________. 아니, 그렇지 않아.

5 A: ____________ James ____________ ____________ ____________ on
Tuesdays? James는 화요일마다 그의 개를 산책시키니?

B: Yes, ____________ ____________. 응, 그래.

6 A: ____________ James ____________ ____________ ____________ on
Wednesdays? James는 수요일마다 자전거를 타니?

B: Yes, ____________ ____________. 응, 그래.

A 우리말과 같은 뜻이 되도록 빈칸에 알맞은 말을 쓰세요.

1 __________ He __________ __________ doesn't __________ __________ wear __________
glasses.
그는 안경을 쓰지 않는다.

2 A: __________ __________ __________
goats?　그들은 염소들을 키우니?
B: __________, __________ __________.
응, 그래.

3 __________ __________ __________ a book
every night.
나는 매일 밤 책을 읽지 않는다.

4 A: __________ __________ __________ a
small bowl?　우리는 작은 그릇이 필요하니?
B: __________, __________ __________.
아니, 그렇지 않아.

5 The apple juice __________ __________
__________.
그 사과 주스는 쓴 맛이 나지 않는다.

6 A: __________ water __________ at 100℃?
물은 섭씨 100도에서 어니?
B: __________, __________ __________.
아니, 그렇지 않아.

B 우리말과 같은 뜻이 되도록 빈칸에 알맞은 말을 쓰세요.

1 _____Do_____ Emily and Dan _____fight_____ every day?

Emily와 Dan은 매일 싸우니?

2 _____________ _____________ _____________ chocolate cake.

그들은 초콜릿 케이크를 좋아하지 않는다.

3 _____________ his fans _____________ _____________?

그의 팬들은 행복하다고 느끼니?

4 We _____________ _____________ _____________.

우리는 일본어를 하지 않는다.

5 _____________ _____________ _____________ this week?

그는 이번 주에 일하니?

6 My friend _____________ _____________ _____________ _____________.

내 친구는 흐린 날들을 좋아하지 않는다.

7 My dogs _____________ _____________ at all.

내 개들은 전혀 짖지 않는다.

8 _____________ _____________ _____________ your bike on Mondays?

너는 월요일마다 자전거를 타니?

9 _____________ _____________ _____________ his old house.

그는 그의 옛 집을 그리워하지 않는다.

10 _____________ your head _____________?

너의 머리가 아프니?

11 You _____________ _____________ very _____________.

너는 그렇게 자주 노래하지 않는다.

12 The _____________ _____________ _____________ a big mouth.

그 괴물은 큰 입을 갖고 있지 않다.

[1~3] 사진을 보고 (   ) 안에서 알맞은 것을 고르세요.

1 

The man (don't play / doesn't play) the guitar.

2 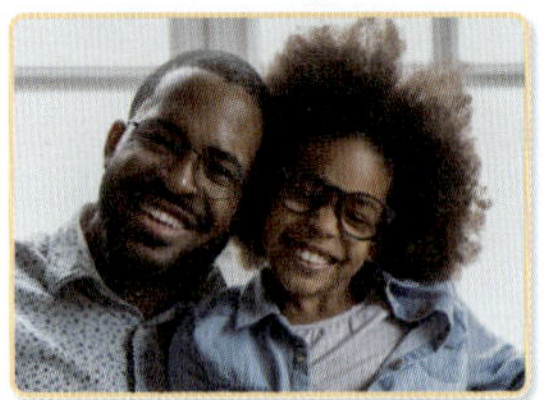

They (wear / don't wear) glasses.

3 

A: Does Emma have blond hair?
B: (Yes, she does. / No, she doesn't.)

[4~5] 빈칸에 들어갈 알맞은 말을 고르세요.

4 ＿＿＿＿＿＿ doesn't eat meat.

① We   ② He   ③ You   ④ I

5 ＿＿＿＿＿＿ you and your brother like hip-hop music?

① Is   ② Are   ③ Do   ④ Does

[6~7] 질문에 대한 대답으로 알맞은 것을 고르세요.

6

Does she know your phone number?

① Yes, she do.　　② Yes, she does.

③ No, she isn't.　　④ No, she don't.

7

A: Do you exercise every day?
B: ＿＿＿＿＿＿ I exercise twice a week.

① Yes, I am.　　② No, I'm not.

③ Yes, I do.　　④ No, I don't.

[8~9] 어법상 올바른 문장을 고르세요.

8　① I don't keep a diary.

② Does they play basketball every day?

③ Do Victoria walk her dog in the morning?

④ The restaurant doesn't sells salad.

9　① Does he wants a new cellphone?

② Paul don't wash the dishes after a meal.

③ It doesn't have a long tail.

④ Does frogs sleep in winter?

10 빈칸에 들어갈 말이 바르게 짝지어진 것을 고르세요.

> · I _____________ have a laptop.
> · _____________ Alex do his homework in the evening?

① don't – Do ② don't – Does

③ doesn't – Do ④ doesn't – Does

11 빈칸에 들어갈 말이 나머지와 <u>다른</u> 것을 고르세요.

① _____________ the store open at 9?

② Lily _____________ not clean her room.

③ I _____________ not like horror movies.

④ _____________ your sister get up early?

12 대화가 <u>어색한</u> 것을 고르세요.

① A: Does Jiwoo speak Japanese?
   B: Yes, she does. She speaks it very well.

② A: Does your dad like shrimp?
   B: No, he doesn't.

③ A: Do you drink coffee at night?
   B: No, I don't.

④ A: Does she teach English?
   B: Yes, she does. She teaches math.

13 다음 문장을 부정문으로 바꿔 쓰세요.

Grace works on weekends.

→ _______________________________________

14 우리말과 같은 뜻이 되도록 주어진 말을 이용하여 문장을 쓰세요.

이 기차는 광주로 가나요? (this train, go to Gwangju)

→ _______________________________________

15 다음 그림을 보고 대화를 완성하세요.

A: Does Peter like vegetables?
B: No, _____________ _____________.
A: Does Anna like vegetables?
B: _____________, _____________ _____________.
A: Do Peter and Anna like meat?
B: _____________, _____________ _____________.

실전 Test 01회

[1~2] 동사원형과 3인칭 단수형이 <u>잘못</u> 짝지어진 것을 고르세요.

1
① pass – passes
② try – tries
③ meet – meets
④ catch – catchs

2
① have – haves
② mix – mixes
③ feel – feels
④ love – loves

[3~4] 빈칸에 들어갈 알맞은 말을 고르세요.

3 My uncle __________ hockey on weekends.

① is
② play
③ are
④ plays

4 __________ doesn't like camping.

① Mom and I
② We
③ Mr. Lee
④ My friends

5 우리말을 영어로 바르게 옮긴 것을 고르세요.

James와 나는 그녀를 잘 알지 못한다.

① James and I know her very well.
② James and I don't know her very well.
③ James and I doesn't know her very well.
④ James and I knows her very well.

[6~7] 빈칸에 들어갈 수 <u>없는</u> 말을 고르세요.

6 Does __________ go swimming after school?

① your brother
② you
③ she
④ Noah

7 Daniel __________ coffee.

① wants
② buys
③ like
④ drinks

8 빈칸에 공통으로 알맞은 말을 고르세요.

> • __________ your parents read the newspaper?
> • Lisa and I __________ not fight.

① Are[are]　　② Do[do]

③ Is[is]　　④ Does[does]

11 질문에 대한 대답으로 알맞은 것을 고르세요.

> Does your dad cook well?

① Yes, he is.

② Yes, he does.

③ No, he don't.

④ No, he isn't.

[9~10] 밑줄 친 부분이 어색한 것을 고르세요.

9 ① She <u>takes</u> a violin lesson on Mondays.

② Minho <u>studies</u> math every day.

③ The store <u>sells</u> fresh fruit.

④ Sean <u>washs</u> his car every Sunday.

[12~13] 빈칸에 들어갈 말이 나머지와 다른 것을 고르세요.

12 ① The bus ______ not go to Seoul.

② ______ he swim well?

③ ______ they have a dog?

④ Amy ______ not eat fast food.

10 ① I don't <u>play</u> computer games.

② <u>Does</u> it snow a lot in Jeju-do?

③ Isabella <u>don't</u> wear skirts.

④ <u>Do</u> they want a new car?

13 ① Jamie ______ not drive a taxi.

② ______ you read at night?

③ I ______ not like loud music.

④ ______ Kevin and Julian play golf?

14

> · She _________ a bath every evening.
> · Rabbits _________ long ears.

① take – have   ② takes – has

③ takes – have   ④ take – has

15

> A: Does Ryan _________ a brother?
> B: No, he _________. He has a sister.

① has – don't   ② have – doesn't

③ has – doesn't   ④ have – don't

16 밑줄 친 부분을 바르게 고친 것을 고르세요.

> · Bora <u>wash</u> her hair every day.
> · Butterflies <u>flies</u> beautifully.

① washs – flys   ② washs – fly

③ washes – flys   ④ washes – fly

17 ① The dog doesn't look healthy.

② Does Rachel cooks well?

③ Babies often cry.

④ We visit our grandparents every month.

18 ① Mom don't drink soda.

② The cat jumps really high.

③ They ride bicycles every morning.

④ I don't wear hats.

19 대화가 <u>어색한</u> 것을 고르세요.

① A: Do they speak English?
　 B: No, they don't.

② A: Do you have a ruler?
　 B: No, I don't.

③ A: Does the flowers smell good?
　 B: Yes, they do.

④ A: Does your son play the piano?
　 B: Yes, he does.

20 다음 문장을 부정문으로 바꿔 쓰세요.

I have long hair now.

➡ ______________________________

____

21 우리말과 같은 뜻이 되도록 주어진 말을 이용하여 문장을 쓰세요.

그 개는 사람을 물지 않는다.
(the dog, bite people)

➡ ______________________________

____

22 다음 문장을 의문문으로 바꿔 쓰고, 그 대답을 완성하세요.

Paul lives in this neighborhood.

➡ A: ______________________________

____

B: Yes, ______________________.

23 다음 그림을 보고 보기 에서 알맞은 단어를 골라 쓰세요. (필요하면 형태를 바꾸세요.)

보기　　open　　sell　　close

(1) The restaurant ____________ pizza.

(2) The restaurant ____________ ____________ on Mondays.

(3) The restaurant ____________ at 9:00 p.m. on Sundays.

be동사의 과거형

학습목표

1 **be**동사 과거형의 형태와 쓰임에 대해 알아보아요.
2 **be**동사의 과거형과 함께 쓰는 표현을 알아보아요.
3 **be**동사 과거형의 부정문을 만드는 법을 알아보아요.
4 **be**동사 과거형의 의문문을 만드는 법을 알아보아요.

nervous
긴장한

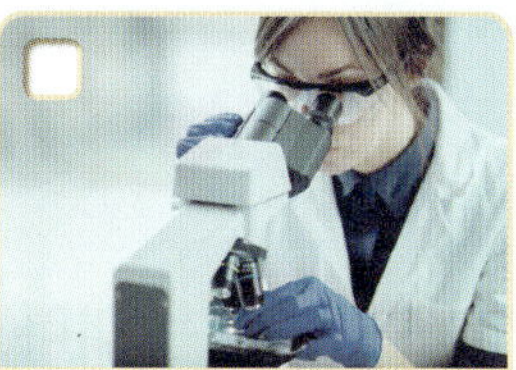

scientist
과학자

zoo
동물원

fresh
신선한

sweet
달콤한

thirsty
목이 마른

army
군대

refrigerator
냉장고

shelf
선반

confident
자신감 있는

heavy
무거운

beach
해변, 바닷가

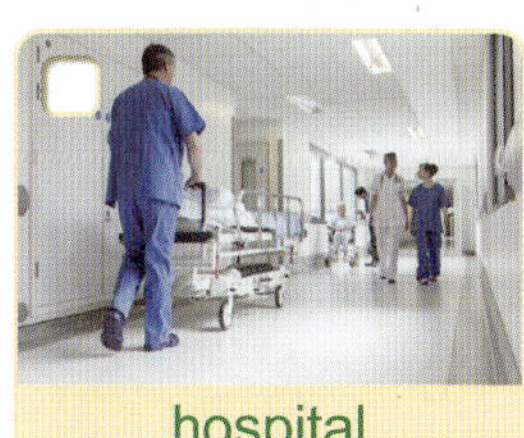

hospital
병원

delicious
맛있는

comfortable
편안한

wallet
지갑

meeting
회의

colorful
(색이) 다채로운

roof
지붕

audience
관객

be동사의 과거형 (1)

● be동사의 현재형으로는 현재의 사실을, be동사의 과거형으로는 이미 지나간 과거의 일을 나타낼 수 있어요.

> Sam **is** a basketball player. Sam은 농구 선수이다. [현재의 사실]
> Sam **was** a basketball player. Sam은 농구 선수였다. [과거의 사실]

● be동사의 과거형은 주어에 따라 was 또는 were 두 가지를 사용해요.

• 주어가 인칭대명사일 때

주어	현재형	과거형
I	am	was
He / She / It	is	
You / We / They	are	were

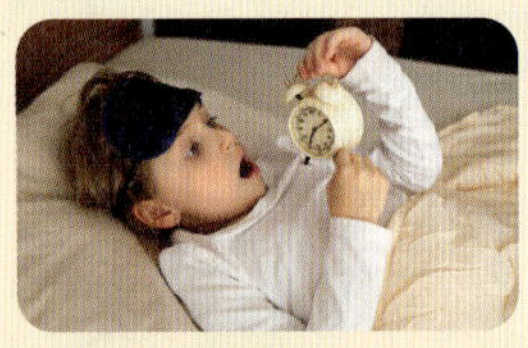

I **was** excited at the concert. 나는 콘서트에서 신이 났다.
She **was** late for school. 그녀는 학교에 늦었다.
They **were** famous actors. 그들은 유명한 배우들이었다.

• 주어가 명사일 때

주어	현재형	과거형
단수명사	is	was
셀 수 없는 명사		
복수명사	are	were

An apple **was** on the table. 사과 하나가 탁자 위에 있었다.
The juice **was** very cold. 그 주스는 매우 차가웠다.
The books **were** interesting. 그 책들은 흥미로웠다.

CHECK UP

A 과거를 나타내는 문장에 V 표시하세요.

1 He was my baseball coach.　그는 나의 야구 코치였다.　

2 Today is moving day.　오늘은 이삿날이다.

3 It was sunny on Saturday.　토요일은 날씨가 맑았다.

4 The street was very dirty.　그 거리는 매우 지저분했다.

5 They are his neighbors.　그들은 그의 이웃들이다.

6 We were nervous at that time.　우리는 그 당시에 긴장했다.

7 I am her best friend.　나는 그녀의 가장 친한 친구이다.

B ( ) 안에서 알맞은 것을 고르세요.

1 She (was / were) a great scientist.　그녀는 훌륭한 괴학지였다.

2 My cats (was / were) sick last week.　지난주에 내 고양이들이 아팠다.

3 It (was / were) rainy last night.　어젯밤에 비가 왔다.

4 They (was / were) excited about the gifts.　그들은 선물들에 신이 났었다.

5 The floor (was / were) clean in the room.　방안의 바닥이 깨끗했다.

6 The movie (was / were) fun.　그 영화는 재미있었다.

7 We (was / were) students at that time.　우리는 그 당시에 학생이었다.

be동사의 과거형 (2)

● be동사의 과거형은 현재형과 마찬가지로 여러 의미로 해석할 수 있어요.

현재형 ~이다 / (~에) 있다 / ~하다	과거형 ~이었다 / (~에) 있었다 / ~했다
I **am** a teacher. 나는 선생님이다.	I **was** a teacher. 나는 선생님이었다.
He **is** at the bank. 그는 은행에 있다.	He **was** at the bank. 그는 은행에 있었다.
They **are** sad. 그들은 슬프다.	They **were** sad. 그들은 슬펐다.

● be동사의 과거형은 과거를 나타내는 표현과 함께 쓸 수 있어요.

last ~ 지난 ~	last night 어젯밤　　　last week 지난주　　　last month[year] 지난달[해]
~ ago ~ 전에	an hour ago 1시간 전에　　　　　a few minutes ago 몇 분 전에
yesterday 어제	yesterday morning 어제 아침　　　the day before yesterday 그저께
in ~ ~년에	in 1910 1910년에　　　in 2014 2014년에
	before 전에　　　at that time 그 당시에　　　then 그때

He **was** busy **last week**. 그는 지난주에 바빴다.
I **was** a singer **10 years ago**. 나는 10년 전에 가수였다.
They **were** in New York **in 2019**. 그들은 2019년에 뉴욕에 있었다.

> **Tip**　be동사의 현재형은 now (지금), right now(지금 (당장)) 같은 표현들과 함께 쓸 수 있어요.
> She is in the kitchen **now**.　그녀는 지금 부엌에 있다. (O)
> She is in the kitchen **yesterday**.　그녀는 어제 부엌에 있다. (X)

CHECK UP

A 다음 중 우리말과 일치하는 문장을 고르세요.

1 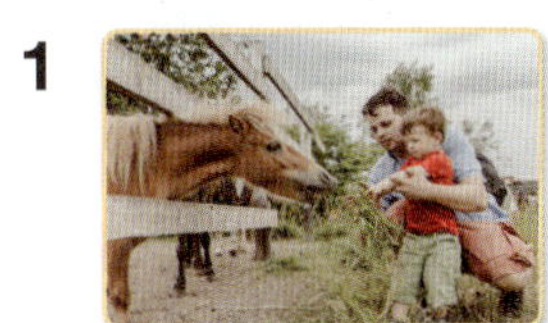

그들은 동물원에 있었다.

ⓐ They are at the zoo.　　ⓑ✓ They were at the zoo.

2 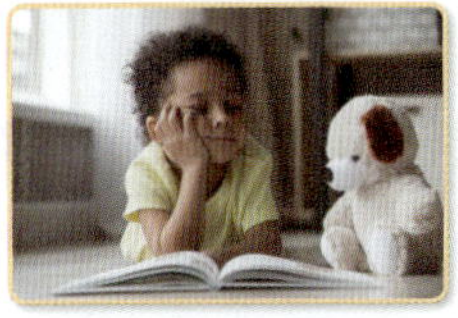

그것은 지루한 책이었다.

ⓐ It is a boring book.　　ⓑ It was a boring book.

3 

어제는 추웠다.

ⓐ Yesterday was cold.　　ⓑ Yesterday is cold.

4 

보라의 생일이었다.

ⓐ It was Bora's birthday.　　ⓑ It is Bora's birthday.

B (　　) 안에서 알맞은 것을 고르세요.

1 She (**is** / was) happy now.　그녀는 지금 행복하다.

2 I (am / was) a fashion model before.　나는 전에 패션 모델이었다.

3 They (are / were) young at that time.　그들은 그 당시에 어렸다.

4 The kids (are / were) in the park now.　그 아이들은 지금 공원에 있다.

5 The milk (is / was) fresh yesterday.　어제 그 우유는 신선했다.

6 Sarah (is / was) a writer a few years ago.　Sarah는 몇 년 전에 작가였다.

주어에 따라 달라지는 be동사
과거형의 형태를 익혀요.

A 빈칸에 들어갈 말로 알맞은 것을 고르세요.

1 They _________ great soccer players.　　ⓐ was　　✓ⓑ were
그들은 훌륭한 축구 선수들이었다.

2 I _________ in the department store.　　ⓐ was　　ⓑ were
나는 백화점에 있었다.

3 The ice cream _________ tasty.　　ⓐ was　　ⓑ were
그 아이스크림은 맛있었다.

4 The leaves _________ green a month ago.　　ⓐ was　　ⓑ were
그 나뭇잎들은 한 달 전에 초록색이었다.

5 It _________ windy yesterday.　　ⓐ was　　ⓑ were
어제 바람이 불었다.

6 The boxes _________ small.　　ⓐ was　　ⓑ were
그 상자들은 작았다.

B 밑줄 친 부분을 바르게 고쳐 쓰세요.

1 The movie <u>were</u> scary.　　→　_____was_____
그 영화는 무서웠다.

2 They <u>was</u> famous writers before.　　→　__________
그들은 전에 유명한 작가들이었다.

3 His desk <u>were</u> clean.　　→　__________
그의 책상은 깨끗했다.

4 They <u>was</u> middle school students.　　→　__________
그들은 중학생이었다.

5 The keys <u>was</u> under the sofa.　　→　__________
그 열쇠들은 소파 아래에 있었다.

LET'S PRACTICE 2

be동사 과거형의 의미와 과거를 나타내는 표현을 익혀요.

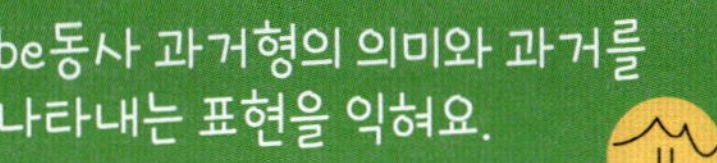

A be동사에 ○ 표시하고 알맞은 우리말 뜻을 고르세요.

1 The cookies (were) sweet.　　　☑ ~했다　ⓑ 있었다

2 The man was a hockey player.　　ⓐ ~이다　ⓑ ~였다

3 They were at the amusement park.　ⓐ ~였다　ⓑ 있었다

4 It is Dave's jacket.　　　　　　ⓐ ~이다　ⓑ ~였다

5 He was at the police station yesterday.　ⓐ ~했다　ⓑ 있었다

6 Richard is kind to everyone.　　ⓐ ~하다　ⓑ ~했다

7 Her socks were in the box.　　　ⓐ 있다　ⓑ 있었다

B 우리말과 같은 뜻이 되도록 보기 에서 알맞은 be동사를 골라 쓰세요. (중복 사용 가능)

보기	is	are	was	were

1 The festival ___was___ boring.　그 축제는 지루했다.

2 She ___________ very busy right now.　그녀는 지금 매우 바쁘다.

3 We ___________ classmates last year.　우리는 작년에 같은 반이었다.

4 They ___________ good teachers.　그들은 좋은 선생님들이었다.

5 Steve ___________ at the gym yesterday.　Steve는 어제 체육관에 있었다.

6 They ___________ at the theater now.　그들은 지금 극장에 있다.

7 I ___________ 10 years old at that time.　나는 그 당시에 10살이었다.

A 빈칸에 알맞은 be동사의 과거형을 쓰세요.

1 The puppies ___were___ in the woods.   강아지들은 숲 속에 있었다.

2 The necklace ___________ my mom's.   그 목걸이는 나의 엄마의 것이었다.

3 My sister ___________ 12 years old last year.   내 여동생은 작년에 12살이었다.

4 The two boys ___________ roommates.   두 소년들은 룸메이트였다.

5 My mom ___________ a doctor before.   나의 엄마는 전에 의사였다.

6 Your notebooks ___________ on the desk.   너의 공책들은 책상 위에 있었다.

7 He ___________ thirsty last night.   그는 어젯밤에 목이 말랐다.

8 The wolves ___________ in the cage.   늑대들은 우리 안에 있었다.

9 He ___________ a cellist at that time.   그는 그 당시에 첼로 연주자였다.

10 They ___________ at the restaurant an hour ago.
그들은 한 시간 전에 식당에 있었다.

11 The steak ___________ salty.   그 스테이크는 짰다.

12 Nate and Jim ___________ shy before.   Nate와 Jim은 전에 수줍음을 많이 탔다.

B ( ) 안에서 알맞은 be동사를 고르고, 과거시제로 바꿔 쓰세요.

1 The food (am / are / is) warm.   그 음식은 따뜻하다.

➡ The food ______was______ warm.

2 These comic books (am / are / is) popular.   이 만화책들은 인기 있다.

➡ These comic books ____________ popular.

3 Her story (am / are / is) interesting.   그녀의 이야기는 흥미롭다.

➡ Her story ____________ interesting.

4 My grandparents (am / are / is) healthy.   나의 조부모님은 건강하시다.

➡ My grandparents ____________ healthy.

5 I (am / are / is) friendly to my neighbors.   나는 내 이웃들에게 친절하다.

➡ I ____________ friendly to my neighbors.

6 The dishes (am / are / is) very dirty.   그 접시들은 매우 지저분하다.

➡ The dishes ____________ very dirty.

7 Red flowers (am / are / is) in my garden.   빨간 꽃들이 나의 정원에 있다.

➡ Red flowers ____________ in my garden.

8 It (am / are / is) my favorite toy.   그것은 내가 가장 좋아하는 장난감이다.

➡ It ____________ my favorite toy.

9 The old castle (am / are / is) really big.   그 오래된 성은 정말 크다.

➡ The old castle ____________ really big.

STEP UP 2

A 빈칸에 공통으로 알맞은 be동사를 쓰세요.

1 The weather _____was_____ good yesterday.   어제 날씨가 좋았다.

She _____was_____ very tired last night.   그녀는 어젯밤에 매우 피곤했다.

2 They ___________ very brave at that time.   그들은 그 당시에 매우 용감했다.

We ___________ in America last year.   우리는 작년에 미국에 있었다.

3 Yesterday ___________ moving day.   어제는 이삿날이었다.

It ___________ cloudy on Sunday.   일요일은 날씨가 흐렸다.

4 I ___________ excited at the festival.   나는 축제에서 신이 났다.

She ___________ a teacher five years ago.   그녀는 5년 전에 선생님이었다.

5 We ___________ in the army at that time.   우리는 그 당시에 군대에 있었다.

They ___________ great handball players.   그들은 훌륭한 핸드볼 선수들이었다.

6 My mom ___________ late for work.   나의 엄마는 회사에 늦었다.

The orange juice ___________ in the refrigerator.   그 오렌지 주스는 냉장고 안에 있었다.

7 My sons ___________ in the park.   내 아들들은 공원에 있었다.

The vegetables ___________ fresh yesterday.   그 채소들은 어제 신선했다.

8 Tim ___________ a singer a few years ago.   Tim은 몇 년 전에 가수였다.

A deer ___________ in the woods.   사슴 한 마리가 숲속에 있었다.

9 The lions ___________ in the cage.   사자들은 우리 안에 있었다.

Her songs ___________ popular.   그녀의 노래는 인기 있었다.

10 The cities ___________ beautiful.   그 도시들은 아름다웠다.

The movie tickets ___________ expensive.   그 영화 티켓들은 비쌌다.

B 사진을 보고 주어진 말을 이용하여 빈칸에 알맞은 말을 쓰세요.

1. Her hands _______were_______ _______cold_______. (cold)
그녀의 손은 차가웠다.

2. The old factory _______________ _______________.
(big)
그 오래된 공장은 컸다.

3. The dishes _______________ _______________.
(clean)
그 접시들은 깨끗했다.

4. My _______________ _______________ under the sofa. (cat)
내 고양이는 소파 아래에 있었다.

5. The girl _______________ _______________ by the gift yesterday. (surprised)
그 소녀는 어제 그 선물에 놀랐다.

6. The _______________ _______________ on the shelf. (plants)
식물들은 선반 위에 있었다.

A 다음 문장을 주어진 주어로 시작하는 문장으로 바꿔 쓰세요.

1 The books were on the desk. 그 책들은 책상 위에 있었다.

→ The milk ______was on the desk______.

2 The waiters were very busy yesterday. 웨이터들은 어제 매우 바빴다.

→ My dad ______________________.

3 Sam was in the department store. Sam은 백화점에 있었다.

→ They ______________________.

4 The watch was my grandmother's. 그 손목시계는 나의 할머니의 것이었다.

→ The rings ______________________.

5 Anna was confident at that time. Anna는 그 당시에 자신감이 있었다.

→ Anna and Bora ______________________.

6 My brother was hungry last night. 나의 남동생은 어젯밤에 배가 고팠다.

→ The boys ______________________.

7 The elephants were in the zoo. 그 코끼리들은 동물원에 있었다.

→ The tiger ______________________.

8 The kids were kind to everyone. 그 아이들은 모두에게 친절했다.

→ My daughter ______________________.

9 My parents were in China before. 나의 부모님은 전에 중국에 계셨다.

→ My sister ______________________.

10 He was very nervous. 그는 매우 긴장했었다.

→ They ______________________.

Ⓑ 밑줄 친 부분을 바르게 고쳐 문장을 다시 쓰세요.

1 I <u>am</u> at the mall the day before yesterday.　나는 그저께 쇼핑몰에 있었다.

➔ ___________ I was at the mall the day before yesterday. ___________

2 They <u>were</u> at the police station now.　그들은 지금 경찰서에 있다.

➔ ____

3 The band <u>is</u> at the festival a month ago.　그 밴드는 한 달 전에 축제에 있었다.

➔ ____

4 Sarah and Anna <u>are</u> neighbors last year.　Sarah와 Anna는 작년에 이웃이었다.

➔ ____

5 My brother <u>was</u> in a restaurant now.　나의 형은 지금 식당에 있다.

➔ ____

6 She <u>were</u> a guitarist at that time.　그녀는 그 당시에 기타 연주자였다.

➔ ____

7 The doctors <u>was</u> in Africa in 2010.　그 의사들은 2010년에 아프리카에 있었다.

➔ ____

8 My cat <u>is</u> on the bed last night.　나의 고양이는 어젯밤에 침대 위에 있었다.

➔ ____

9 The boys <u>was</u> best friends before.　그 소년들은 전에 단짝 친구였다.

➔ ____

10 I <u>was</u> at the amusement park right now.　나는 지금 놀이공원에 있다.

➔ ____

STEP UP 4

 A ( ) 안의 말을 문장 끝에 덧붙여 과거시제 문장으로 바꿔 쓰세요.

1 It is snowy. (last night) 눈이 내린다.

→ _______________ It was snowy last night. _______________

2 The water is very cold. (an hour ago) 물이 매우 차갑다.

→ ____

3 My puppies are sick. (last month) 내 강아지들이 아프다.

→ ____

4 They are kids. (at that time) 그들은 아이들이다.

→ ____

5 His room is clean. (yesterday morning) 그의 방은 깨끗하다.

→ ____

6 They are elementary school students. (in 2020) 그들은 초등학생들이다.

→ ____

7 The girl is a soccer player. (a few years ago) 그 소녀는 축구 선수이다.

→ ____

8 My nephew is 11 years old. (last year) 내 조카는 11살이다.

→ ____

9 The men are famous artists. (before) 그 남자들은 유명한 화가들이다.

→ ____

10 Your shoes are under the bed. (a few minutes ago) 너의 신발은 침대 아래에 있다.

→ ____

B 그림을 보고 보기 에서 알맞은 말을 골라 be동사와 함께 쓰세요.

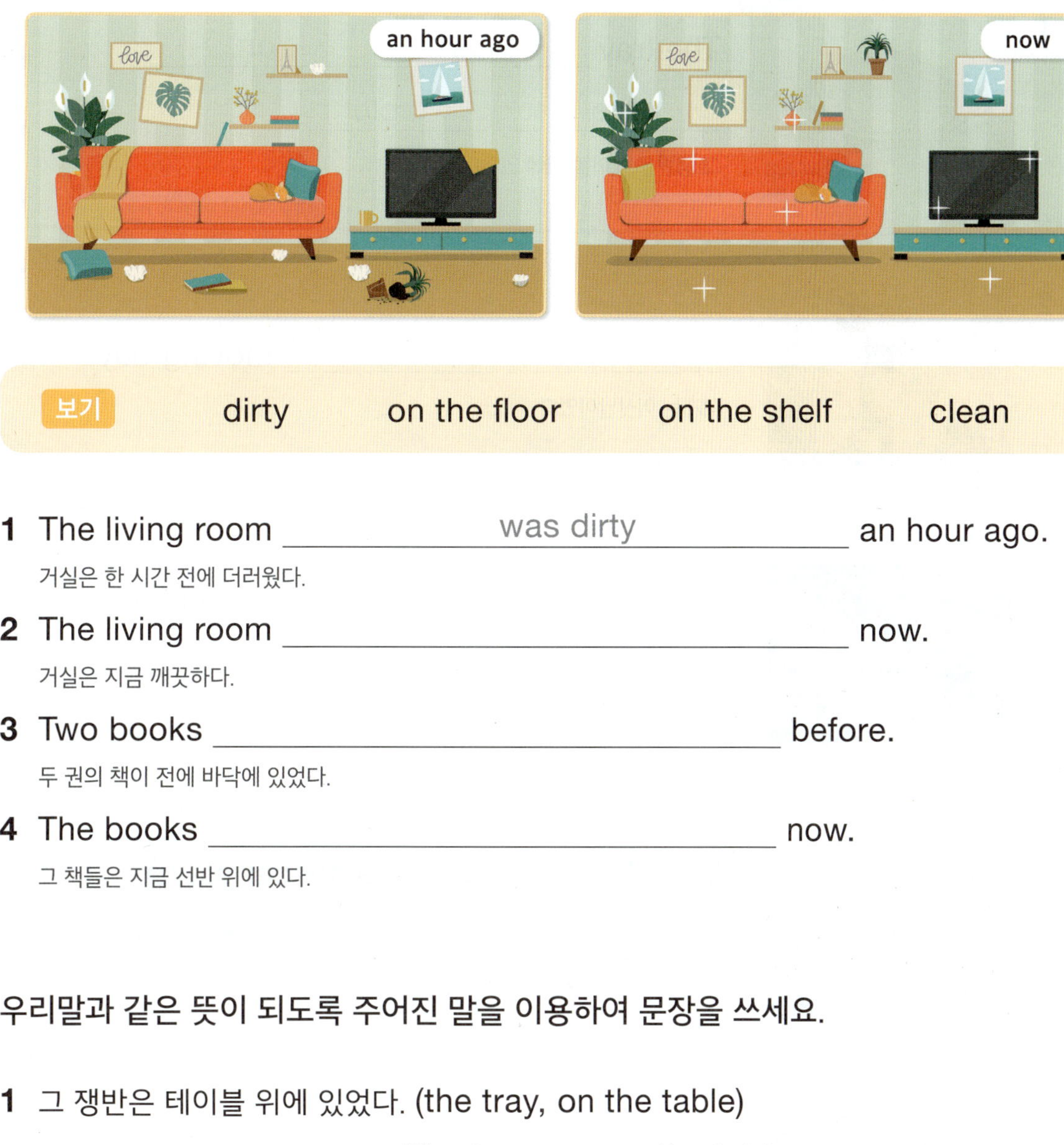

보기　　dirty　　　on the floor　　　on the shelf　　　clean

1 The living room ________was dirty________ an hour ago.
거실은 한 시간 전에 더러웠다.

2 The living room ________________________ now.
거실은 지금 깨끗하다.

3 Two books ________________________ before.
두 권의 책이 전에 바닥에 있었다.

4 The books ________________________ now.
그 책들은 지금 선반 위에 있다.

C 우리말과 같은 뜻이 되도록 주어진 말을 이용하여 문장을 쓰세요.

1 그 쟁반은 테이블 위에 있었다. (the tray, on the table)

→ ________The tray was on the table.________

2 그 새로운 게임은 재미있었다. (the new game, fun)

→ ________________________

3 그녀의 이야기들은 무서웠다. (her stories, scary)

→ ________________________

4 저것들은 내가 가장 좋아하는 인형들이었다. (those, my favorite dolls)

→ ________________________

A 우리말과 같은 뜻이 되도록 빈칸에 알맞은 말을 쓰세요.

1

The tray ___was___ ___on___ ___the___ ___table___.
그 쟁반은 테이블 위에 있었다.

2

______________ ______________ moving day.
어제는 이삿날이었다.

3

The ______________ ______________ in the ______________.
그 코끼리들은 동물원에 있었다.

4

The girl ______________ a soccer player ______________ ______________ years ago.
그 소녀는 몇 년 전에 축구 선수였다.

5

The ______________ ______________ ______________ a month ago.
그 나뭇잎들은 한 달 전에 초록색이었다.

6

______________ ______________ at the theater ______________.
그들은 지금 극장에 있다.

B 우리말과 같은 뜻이 되도록 빈칸에 알맞은 말을 쓰세요.

1 My brother ___________ was ___________ hungry ___________ last ___________ night ___________ .
나의 남동생은 어젯밤에 배가 고팠다.

2 It ___________ ___________ on ___________ .
일요일은 날씨가 흐렸다.

3 ___________ ___________ ___________ at that time.
우리는 그 당시에 긴장했다.

4 My cats ___________ ___________ ___________ ___________ .
지난주에 내 고양이들이 아팠다.

5 His ___________ ___________ ___________ yesterday morning.
그의 방은 어제 아침에 깨끗했다.

6 Sarah ___________ ___________ ___________ a few years ago.
Sarah는 몇 년 전에 작가였다.

7 The ___________ ___________ ___________ .
그 쿠키들은 달콤했다.

8 I ___________ 10 years old ___________ ___________ ___________ .
나는 그 당시에 10살이었다.

9 The ___________ ___________ ___________ mom's.
그 목걸이는 나의 엄마의 것이었다.

10 The kids ___________ in the ___________ ___________ .
그 아이들은 지금 공원에 있다.

11 ___________ ___________ ___________ scary.
그녀의 이야기들은 무서웠다.

12 ___________ ___________ at the ___________ ___________ right now.
나는 지금 놀이공원에 있다.

be동사 과거형의 부정문

- **be동사 과거형의 부정문은 was 또는 were 뒤에 not을 붙여서 「주어 + was[were] + not ~」으로 써요.**

It **was** snowy yesterday.
어제는 눈이 내렸다.

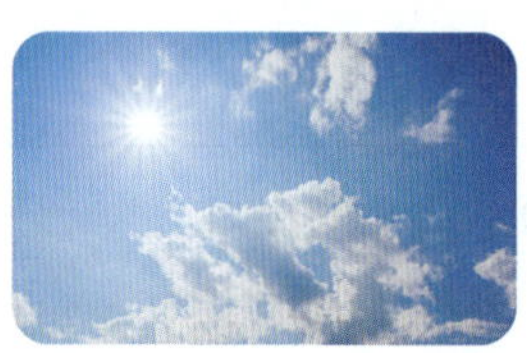
It **was not** snowy yesterday.
어제는 눈이 내리지 않았다.

They **were** in the classroom.
그들은 교실에 있었다.

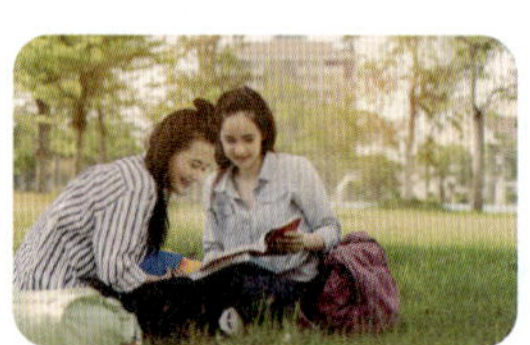
They **were not** in the classroom.
그들은 교실에 있지 않았다.

- **was not은 wasn't로 줄여 쓸 수 있어요.**

My sister **wasn't** bored. 내 여동생은 지루해하지 않았다.
The juice **wasn't** fresh. 그 주스는 신선하지 않았다.
The book **wasn't** on your desk. 그 책은 네 책상 위에 없었다.

- **were not은 weren't로 줄여 쓸 수 있어요.**

You **weren't** in Busan yesterday. 너는 어제 부산에 있지 않았다.
The flowers **weren't** beautiful. 그 꽃들은 아름답지 않았다.
We **weren't** rude at that time. 우리는 그 당시에 무례하지 않았다.

CHECK UP

A be동사의 부정문에 V 표시하세요.

1 The test was not difficult. 그 시험은 어렵지 않았다. 

2 His mom was angry at him. 그의 엄마는 그에게 화가 나셨다. 

3 The weather was not bad yesterday. 어제 날씨는 나쁘지 않았다. 

4 They were in Seoul last week. 그들은 지난주에 서울에 있었다.

5 The shirts were my brother's. 그 셔츠들은 내 형의 것이었다.

6 The movie was not boring. 그 영화는 지루하지 않았다.

7 The students were not absent. 그 학생들은 결석하지 않았다.

B 부정문으로 바꿀 때 not이 들어갈 위치를 고르세요.

1 I ⓐ was ⓑ tired ⓒ last night. 나는 어젯밤에 피곤했다.

2 My parents ⓐ were ⓑ at home ⓒ last weekend. 나의 부모님은 지난 주말에 집에 계셨다.

3 Sarah and ⓐ Jim ⓑ were ⓒ in the same class. Sarah와 Jim은 같은 반이었다.

4 He ⓐ was ⓑ sick ⓒ yesterday. 그는 어제 아팠다.

5 She ⓐ was ⓑ an artist ⓒ before. 그녀는 전에 화가였다.

6 The vegetables ⓐ were ⓑ fresh ⓒ last week. 그 채소들은 지난주에 신선했다.

7 Dan ⓐ was ⓑ 12 years old ⓒ last year. Dan은 작년에 12살이었다.

be동사 과거형의 의문문

● be동사 과거형의 의문문은 「Was[Were] + 주어 ~?」로 나타내요.

• 주어가 단수일 때

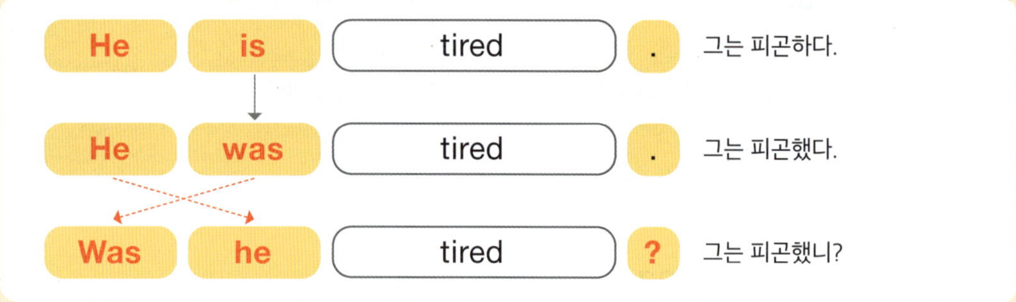

He	is	tired	.	그는 피곤하다.
He	was	tired	.	그는 피곤했다.
Was	he	tired	?	그는 피곤했니?

• 주어가 2인칭(You) 또는 복수일 때

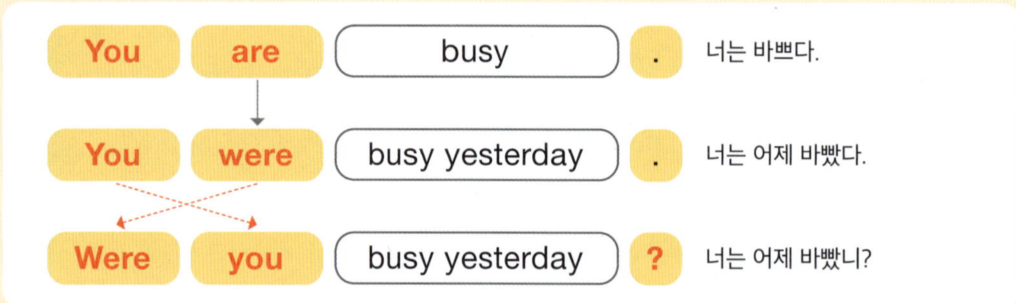

You	are	busy	.	너는 바쁘다.
You	were	busy yesterday	.	너는 어제 바빴다.
Were	you	busy yesterday	?	너는 어제 바빴니?

● 의문문에 대한 긍정 대답은 「Yes, 주어 + was[were].」, 부정 대답은 「No, 주어 + wasn't[weren't].」 의 형태예요.

Was the bag heavy? 그 가방은 무거웠니?
Yes, it **was**. / **No**, it **wasn't**.
응, 그랬어.　　　아니, 그렇지 않았어.

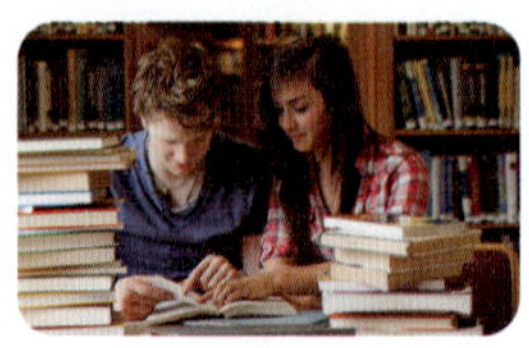

Were they at the library? 그들은 도서관에 있었니?
Yes, they **were**. / **No**, they **weren't**.
응, 그랬어.　　　아니, 그렇지 않았어.

CHECK UP

A 빈칸에 들어갈 말로 알맞은 것을 고르세요.

1 __________ the actor popular before? ⓐ Was ✓ ⓑ Were
그 배우는 전에 인기가 있었니?

2 __________ they at the bank? ⓐ Was ⓑ Were
그들은 은행에 있었니?

3 __________ the waiters kind to you? ⓐ Was ⓑ Were
웨이터들은 너에게 친절했니?

4 __________ the food great there? ⓐ Was ⓑ Were
그곳의 음식은 훌륭했니?

5 __________ they in Italy in 2019? ⓐ Was ⓑ Were
그들은 2019년에 이탈리아에 있었니?

B ( ) 안에서 알맞은 것을 고르세요.

1 
A: Was it snowy yesterday? 어제 눈이 왔니?
B: No, it (was / wasn't). 아니, 그렇지 않았어.

2 
A: Were they soccer players? 그들은 축구 선수들이었니?
B: (Yes / No), they weren't. 아니, 그렇지 않았어.

3 
A: (Was / Were) the kids happy? 그 아이들은 행복했니?
B: Yes, they (were / weren't). 응, 그랬어.

4 
A: (Was / Were) you at the beach? 너는 바닷가에 있었니?
B: (Yes / No), I was. 응, 그랬어.

A (   ) 안에서 알맞은 것을 고르고 그 부분을 축약형으로 쓰세요.

1 The comic book (was not / were not) funny. → _____wasn't_____

그 만화책은 재미있지 않았다.

2 We (was not / were not) busy yesterday. → _____________

우리는 어제 바쁘지 않았다.

3 She (was not / were not) alone then. → _____________

그녀는 그때 혼자가 아니었다.

4 The kids (was not / were not) in the hospital last week. → _____________

그 아이들은 지난주에 병원에 있지 않았다.

5 The pasta (was not / were not) warm enough. → _____________

그 파스타는 충분히 따뜻하지 않았다.

B 밑줄 친 부분을 바르게 고쳐 쓰세요.

1 The books <u>wasn't</u> expensive. → _____weren't[were not]_____

그 책들은 비싸지 않았다.

2 I <u>am not</u> a baseball player two years ago. → _____________

나는 2년 전에 야구 선수가 아니었다.

3 My brother <u>weren't</u> tall last year. → _____________

나의 형은 작년에 키가 크지 않았다.

4 They <u>wasn't</u> good at math. → _____________

그들은 수학을 잘하지 못했다.

5 It <u>weren't</u> cloudy in Seoul yesterday. → _____________

어제 서울은 흐리지 않았다.

6 We <u>aren't</u> friends three years ago. → _____________

우리는 3년 전에 친구가 아니었다.

LET'S PRACTICE 2

be동사 과거형의 의문문과 의문문에 대한 대답을 연습해요.

A 빈칸에 알맞은 be동사를 쓰세요.

1 __________ Was __________ the bread delicious? 그 빵은 맛있었니?

2 __________________ you at home last night? 너는 어젯밤에 집에 있었니?

3 __________________ the bags old? 그 가방들은 낡았었니?

4 __________________ his new book interesting? 그의 새 책은 흥미로웠니?

5 __________________ the weather warm yesterday? 어제 날씨는 따뜻했니?

6 __________________ they good at English at that time? 그들은 그 당시에 영어를 잘했니?

B 빈칸에 알맞은 말을 넣어 대화를 완성하세요.

1 A: Were they in school? 그들은 학교에 있었니?
B: Yes, they __________ were __________. 응, 그랬어.

2 A: Was Jim absent from school yesterday? Jim은 어제 학교에 결석했니?
B: No, he __________________. 아니, 그렇지 않았어.

3 A: Was the science test easy? 과학 시험은 쉬웠니?
B: No, it __________________. 아니, 그렇지 않았어.

4 A: Were the tables clean this morning? 오늘 아침에 탁자들이 깨끗했니?
B: Yes, they __________________. 응, 그랬어.

5 A: Were your parents here an hour ago? 너의 부모님은 한 시간 전에 이곳에 계셨니?
B: No, they __________________. 아니, 그렇지 않으셨어.

6 A: Was the new sofa comfortable? 새 소파는 편안했니?
B: Yes, it __________________. 응, 그랬어.

STEP UP 1

Ⓐ 빈칸에 알맞은 be동사의 과거형을 쓰고, 축약형을 사용하여 부정문으로 바꾸세요.

1 He _______was_______ a math teacher. 그는 수학 선생님이었다.

→ He ______wasn't______ a math teacher. 그는 수학 선생님이 아니었다.

2 They _____________ polite to their parents. 그들은 부모님께 공손했다.

→ They _____________ polite to their parents. 그들은 부모님께 공손하지 않았다.

3 The tomato _____________ fresh. 그 토마토는 신선했다.

→ The tomato _____________ fresh. 그 토마토는 신선하지 않았다.

4 The shoes _____________ small for him. 그 신발은 그에게 작았다.

→ The shoes _____________ small for him. 그 신발은 그에게 작지 않았다.

5 She _____________ a designer at that time. 그녀는 그 당시에 디자이너였다.

→ She _____________ a designer at that time. 그녀는 그 당시에 디자이너가 아니었다.

6 The wallet _____________ here before. 그 지갑은 전에 여기에 있었다.

→ The wallet _____________ here before. 그 지갑은 전에 여기에 있지 않았다.

7 The birds _____________ in a tree. 그 새들은 나무에 있었다.

→ The birds _____________ in a tree. 그 새들은 나무에 있지 않았다.

8 Her friends _____________ on the beach. 그녀의 친구들은 해변에 있었다.

→ Her friends _____________ on the beach. 그녀의 친구들은 해변에 있지 않았다.

9 The boy _____________ smart. 그 소년은 똑똑했다.

→ The boy _____________ smart. 그 소년은 똑똑하지 않았다.

B 빈칸에 알맞은 말을 써서 의문문으로 바꾸세요.

1 She was in Paris in 2019.　그녀는 2019년에 파리에 있었다.

→ _______Was she_______ in Paris in 2019?　그녀는 2019년에 파리에 있었니?

2 The actors were famous before.　그 배우들은 전에 유명했다.

→ _________________________ famous before?　그 배우들은 전에 유명했니?

3 You were late for the meeting this morning.　너는 오늘 아침에 회의에 늦었다.

→ _________________________ late for the meeting this morning?
너는 오늘 아침에 회의에 늦었니?

4 My sister was angry yesterday.　나의 누나는 어제 화가 났었다.

→ _________________________ angry yesterday?　나의 누나는 어제 화가 났었니?

5 James was a basketball player two years ago.　James는 2년 전에 농구 선수였다.

→ _________________________ a basketball player two years ago?
James는 2년 전에 농구 선수였니?

6 The puppies were healthy.　그 강아지들은 건강했다.

→ _________________________ healthy?　그 강아지들은 건강했니?

7 The living room was clean yesterday.　거실은 어제 깨끗했다.

→ _________________________ clean yesterday?　거실은 어제 깨끗했니?

8 The students were on the school bus.　학생들은 스쿨버스에 타고 있었다.

→ _________________________ on the school bus?
학생들은 스쿨버스에 타고 있었니?

A 우리말과 같은 뜻이 되도록 빈칸에 공통으로 알맞은 말을 쓰세요.

1 _____Were_____ they at the museum? 그들은 박물관에 있었니?

The rooms _____were_____ not clean last week. 지난주에 방들은 깨끗하지 않았다.

2 He _____________ angry at me. 그는 나에게 화가 나지 않았다.

The chair _____________ light. 그 의자는 가볍지 않았다.

3 They _____________ at home last night. 그들은 어젯밤에 집에 있지 않았다.

We _____________ nervous at that time. 우리는 그 당시에 긴장되지 않았다.

4 _____________ the pizza warm enough? 피자는 충분히 따뜻했니?

_____________ the computer expensive? 그 컴퓨터는 비쌌니?

5 I _____________ good at English. 나는 영어를 잘하지 못했다.

It _____________ snowy in Busan last winter. 지난 겨울에 부산에는 눈이 내리지 않았다.

6 The students _____________ late for the class. 학생들은 수업에 지각하지 않았다.

The shirts _____________ big for her. 그 셔츠들은 그녀에게 크지 않았다.

7 A: _____________ the new bed comfortable? 새 침대는 편했니?

B: Yes, it _____________. 응, 그랬어.

8 A: _____________ the kids excited? 그 아이들은 신이 났었니?

B: Yes, they _____________. 응, 그랬어.

9 You _____________ not in Jeju-do yesterday. 너는 어제 제주도에 있지 않았다.

The flowers _____________ not colorful. 그 꽃들은 색이 다채롭지 않았다.

10 _____________ the writer popular before? 그 작가는 전에 인기가 있었니?

_____________ the food delicious there? 그곳의 음식은 맛있었니?

B 사진을 보고 빈칸에 알맞은 말을 쓰세요.

1

A: Were they basketball players?
그들은 농구 선수들이었니?
B: No, _____they_____ _____weren't_____.
아니, 그렇지 않았어.

2

She _____________ _____________ an English teacher.
그녀는 영어 선생님이 아니었다.

3

A: Were the vegetables fresh?
그 채소들은 신선했니?
B: _____________, they _____________.
응, 그랬어.

4

The shoes _____________ big for him.
그 신발은 그에게 크지 않았다.

5

The bird _____________ on the roof.
그 새는 지붕 위에 있지 않았다.

6

A: _____________ you late for class this morning?
너는 오늘 아침에 수업에 늦었니?
B: Yes, I _____________.
응, 그랬어.

A 밑줄 친 부분이 맞으면 ○ 표시하고, 틀리면 바르게 고쳐 쓰세요.

1 They <u>wasn't</u> polite to their teacher.   →   <u>weren't[were not]</u>
그들은 선생님께 공손하지 않았다.

2 A: Were your friends here an hour ago?   →   _______________
    너의 친구들은 한 시간 전에 이곳에 있었니?
  B: No, they <u>were</u>.   아니, 그렇지 않았어.

3 She <u>wasn't</u> a comedian at that time.   →   _______________
그녀는 그 당시에 코미디언이 아니었다.

4 <u>Was</u> the animals healthy?   →   _______________
그 동물들은 건강했니?

5 <u>Was</u> your room clean yesterday?   →   _______________
네 방은 어제 깨끗했니?

6 Dan <u>weren't</u> 10 years old last year.   →   _______________
Dan은 작년에 10살이 아니었다.

7 A: <u>Was</u> the desk heavy?   그 책상은 무거웠니?   →   _______________
  B: Yes, it <u>were</u>.   응, 그랬어.

8 <u>Were</u> they good at Spanish at that time?   →   _______________
그들은 그 당시에 스페인어를 잘했니?

9 The backpack <u>weren't</u> here before.   →   _______________
그 가방은 전에 여기에 있지 않았다.

10 A: <u>Were</u> you at a café?   너는 카페에 있었니?   →   _______________
    B: Yes, I <u>were</u>.   응, 그랬어.

B 밑줄 친 부분을 바르게 고쳐 문장을 다시 쓰세요. (부정문은 축약형으로 쓰세요.)

1 Sarah and Jim <u>wasn't</u> in the same class.   Sarah와 Jim은 같은 반이 아니었다.

➡ _______ Sarah and Jim weren't in the same class. _______

2 <u>Were</u> she at the meeting yesterday?   그녀는 어제 회의에 있었니?

➡ _______________________________________

3 The musical <u>weren't</u> funny.   그 뮤지컬은 재미있지 않았다.

➡ _______________________________________

4 <u>Was</u> they in Korea in 2018?   그들은 2018년에 한국에 있었니?

➡ _______________________________________

5 The directors <u>aren't</u> famous before.   그 감독들은 전에 유명하지 않았다.

➡ _______________________________________

6 <u>Was</u> the students on the train?   학생들은 기차에 타고 있었니?

➡ _______________________________________

7 The comic book <u>not was</u> on your desk.   그 만화책은 네 책상 위에 없었다.

➡ _______________________________________

8 We <u>aren't</u> tired yesterday.   우리는 어제 피곤하지 않았다.

➡ _______________________________________

9 <u>Were</u> Dan at home last night?   Dan은 어젯밤에 집에 있었니?

➡ _______________________________________

10 The turtles <u>wasn't</u> on the beach.   그 거북이들은 해변에 있지 않았다.

➡ _______________________________________

STEP UP 4

A 다음 문장을 주어진 지시대로 바꿔 쓰세요. (부정문은 축약형으로 쓰세요.)

1 My coach was busy yesterday. (부정문) 나의 코치는 어제 바빴다.

→ My coach wasn't busy yesterday.

2 You were in the hospital last week. (의문문) 너는 지난주에 병원에 있었다.

→ ______________________________________

3 They were in Busan last month. (부정문) 그들은 지난달에 부산에 있었다.

→ ______________________________________

4 The skirt was my sister's. (부정문) 그 치마는 내 누나의 것이었다.

→ ______________________________________

5 Tom was a baseball player two years ago. (의문문) Tom은 2년 전에 야구 선수였다.

→ ______________________________________

6 My brother was in Europe last year. (부정문) 나의 남동생은 작년에 유럽에 있었다.

→ ______________________________________

7 The movie was interesting. (의문문) 그 영화는 흥미로웠다.

→ ______________________________________

8 Your parents were in Paris in 2019. (의문문) 너의 부모님은 2019년에 파리에 있었다.

→ ______________________________________

9 The weather was windy yesterday. (부정문) 어제 날씨는 바람이 많이 불었다.

→ ______________________________________

10 Those artists were actors before. (의문문) 저 예술가들은 전에 배우들이었다.

→ ______________________________________

B 우리말과 같은 뜻이 되도록 주어진 말을 이용하여 문장을 완성하세요.

1 그 사과들은 지난주에 신선하지 않았다. (the apples, fresh)

➡ <u>The apples were not[weren't] fresh</u> last week.

2 그는 너에게 친절했니? (kind)

➡ ________________________________ to you?

3 나는 그때 혼자가 아니었다. (alone)

➡ ________________________________ then.

4 그 소파는 저렴하지 않았다. (cheap)

➡ The sofa ________________________________.

5 그들의 이야기들이 지루했니? (their stories)

➡ ________________________________ boring?

C 우리말과 같은 뜻이 되도록 주어진 말을 바르게 배열하세요.

1 그 고양이는 똑똑하지 않았다. (was / smart / not)

➡ The cat <u>was not smart</u>.

2 그 아이들은 학교에 결석했니? (the kids / were / absent)

➡ ________________________________ from school?

3 너는 어제 피곤했니? (were / tired / you)

➡ ________________________________ yesterday?

4 관객은 지루해하지 않았다. (not / bored / was)

➡ The audience ________________________________.

5 그녀는 한 시간 전에 지하철에 있었니? (she / on the subway / was)

➡ ________________________________ an hour ago?

LEVEL UP

 우리말과 같은 뜻이 되도록 빈칸에 알맞은 말을 쓰세요.

1

The movie ___________ was ___________ not
___________ boring .

그 영화는 지루하지 않았다.

2

A: ___________ the ___________ delicious?

그 빵은 맛있었니?

B: Yes, it ___________ . 응, 그랬어.

3

___________ ___________ ___________
___________ last year.

나의 형은 작년에 키가 크지 않았다.

4

A: ___________ they ___________ ___________?

그들은 축구 선수들이었니?

B: No, ___________ ___________ . 아니, 그렇지 않았어.

5

The ___________ ___________ in the hospital
___________ ___________ .

그 아이들은 지난주에 병원에 있지 않았다.

6

___________ his ___________ ___________
interesting?

그의 새 책은 흥미로웠니?

B 우리말과 같은 뜻이 되도록 빈칸에 알맞은 말을 쓰세요.

1 __________ __________ good at English __________ __________ __________ ? 그들은 그 당시에 영어를 잘했니?

2 The __________ __________ __________ .
그 토마토는 신선하지 않았다.

3 __________ the weather __________ __________ ?
어제 날씨는 따뜻했니?

4 __________ __________ __________ yesterday.
우리는 어제 바쁘지 않았다.

5 A: __________ the new __________ comfortable? 새 침대는 편했니?
 B: Yes, __________ __________ . 응, 그랬어.

6 The flowers __________ __________ __________ .
그 꽃들은 색이 다채롭지 않았다.

7 She __________ a __________ at that time.
그녀는 그 당시에 코미디언이 아니었다.

8 A: __________ the __________ happy? 그 아이들은 행복했니?
 B: Yes, __________ __________ . 응, 그랬어.

9 The __________ __________ __________ . 그 학생들은 결석하지 않았다.

10 The backpack __________ __________ __________ .
그 가방은 전에 여기에 있지 않았다.

11 __________ the tables clean __________ __________ ?
오늘 아침에 탁자들이 깨끗했니?

12 __________ the desk __________ ? 그 책상은 무거웠니?

[1~3] (   ) 안에서 알맞은 be동사를 고르고, 과거시제로 바꿔 쓰세요.

1 We (am / is / are) in Paris. ➡ We ______________ in Paris.

2 The wind (am / is / are) very strong. ➡ The wind ____________ very strong.

3 (Am / Is / Are) you at the museum? ➡ ____________ you at the museum?

4 다음 문장에서 not이 들어갈 위치를 고르세요.

> My dad ① was ② a police officer ③ before ④.

5 빈칸에 들어갈 말이 바르게 짝지어진 것을 고르세요.

> • ______________ you late for work now?
> • The math test ____________ not easy yesterday.

① Are – is   ② Were – is   ③ Are – was   ④ Were – was

6 우리말을 영어로 바르게 옮긴 것을 고르세요.

> 그 배우는 그 당시에 부유하지 않았다.

① The actor isn't rich at that time.

② The actor aren't rich at that time.

③ The actor wasn't rich at that time.

④ The actor weren't rich at that time.

7 빈칸에 들어갈 말이 나머지와 <u>다른</u> 것을 고르세요.

① We ____________ really busy last week.

② ____________ you and Nick at the mall last Saturday?

③ They ____________ very nervous at that time.

④ The weather ____________ really nice yesterday.

8 대화가 <u>어색한</u> 것을 고르세요.

① A: Was the test difficult?
   B: Yes, they were.

② A: Were the bags big?
   B: No, they weren't.

③ A: Was Sam in Korea last month?
   B: Yes, he was.

④ A: Were you free yesterday?
   B: No, I wasn't.

9 빈칸에 들어갈 수 <u>없는</u> 말을 고르세요.

> Sophia was in Seoul _____________.

① in 2020　　② a week ago　　③ right now　　④ last year

10 밑줄 친 부분이 올바른 것을 고르세요.

① The pasta <u>weren't</u> salty.

② She <u>was</u> born in Korea.

③ The pants <u>wasn't</u> mine.

④ <u>Was</u> they best friends before?

11 어법상 <u>틀린</u> 문장을 고르세요.

① Were your parents at home yesterday?

② The strawberries were not fresh.

③ Was Jackson at the library that day?

④ The song were not popular.

12 밑줄 친 부분의 의미가 나머지와 <u>다른</u> 것을 고르세요.

① Your glasses <u>were</u> on the chair.

② My aunt <u>was</u> a teacher before.

③ James <u>was</u> in London last year.

④ They <u>were</u> in the classroom then.

13 다음 문장을 부정문으로 바꿔 쓰세요.

I was sleepy at that time.

➡ ____

14 어법상 <u>틀린</u> 부분을 찾아 바르게 고쳐 쓰세요.

Were the music loud last night?

______________________ ➡ ______________________

15 다음 그림을 보고 빈칸에 알맞은 말을 쓰세요. (부정문은 축약형으로 쓰세요.)

Andy ______________ an elementary school student two years ago. He ______________ tall at that time. Now he ______________ a middle school student. And he ______________ tall.

Chapter 04

There + be동사

Unit 01 「There + be동사」의 현재형과 과거형

Unit 02 「There + be동사」의 부정문과 의문문

학습목표

1 「There + be동사」의 의미와 쓰임을 알아보아요.
2 「There + be동사」의 현재형과 과거형을 알아보아요.
3 「There + be동사」의 부정문과 의문문을 알아보아요.

모르는 단어에 체크해 보세요.

toothbrush
칫솔

basket
바구니

farm
농장

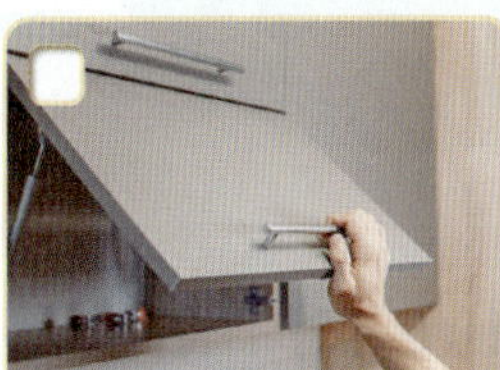
cupboard
찬장

vase
꽃병

subway
지하철

customer
고객

tourist
관광객

palace
궁전

drawer
서랍

playground
놀이터

pond
연못

closet
옷장

dust
먼지

plant
식물

ladder
사다리

fishbowl
어항

clothes
옷

trash can
쓰레기통

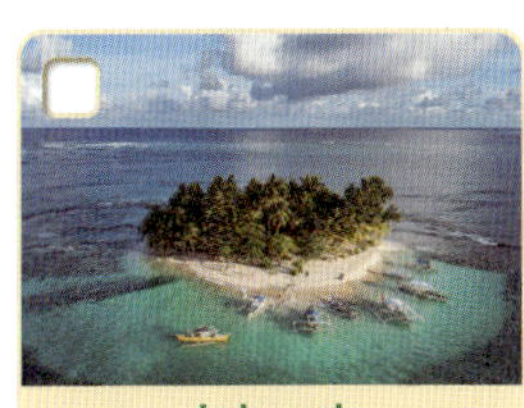
island
섬

「There + be동사」의 현재형과 과거형

● **There is와 There are는 '~가 있다'라는 뜻이며 여기서 There는 따로 해석하지 않아요.**

There is a sofa in the room. 방에 소파가 있다.
There is tea in the cup. 컵 안에 차가 있다.
There are toothbrushes on the shelf. 선반 위에 칫솔들이 있다.

● **There is 뒤에는 단수명사 또는 셀 수 없는 명사가, There are 뒤에는 복수명사가 올 수 있어요.**

There is	단수명사	**There is** a smartphone in my pocket. 내 주머니 안에 스마트폰이 있다. **There is** an onion in the refrigerator. 냉장고 안에 양파가 있다.
	셀 수 없는 명사	**There is** milk in the cup. 컵 안에 우유가 있다. **There is** coffee on the table. 탁자 위에 커피가 있다.
There are	복수명사	**There are** many books. 많은 책들이 있다. **There are** two tables. 탁자 두 개가 있다.

● **There is와 There are의 과거형은 There was 또는 There were로 쓰며 '~가 있었다'로 해석해요.**

There was	단수명사	**There was** a pencil on the desk. 책상 위에 연필이 있었다. **There was** a dog on the sofa. 소파 위에 개 한 마리가 있었다.
	셀 수 없는 명사	**There was** juice in the bottle. 병 안에 주스가 있었다. **There was** salt in the bowl. 그릇 안에 소금이 있었다.
There were	복수명사	**There were** oranges in the basket. 바구니 안에 오렌지들이 있었다. **There were** birds in the tree. 나무에 새들이 있었다.

Tip  There is와 There are는 장소나 위치를 나타내는 말과 자주 쓰여요.

There is a train station **in this town.** 이 동네에는 기차역이 있다.
There are books **on your desk.** 네 책상 위에 책들이 있다.

CHECK UP

A 빈칸에 들어갈 말로 알맞은 것을 고르세요.

1 

There are ______.

장미들이 있다.

ⓐ a rose ⓑ roses

2 

There is ______.

사과가 하나 있다.

ⓐ an apple ⓑ apples

3 

There are ______.

아이들이 있다.

ⓐ a kid ⓑ kids

4 

There is ______.

말이 한 마리 있다.

ⓐ a horse ⓑ horses

5 

There are ______.

나뭇잎들이 있다.

ⓐ a leaf ⓑ leaves

6

There is ______.

토끼가 한 마리 있다.

ⓐ a rabbit ⓑ rabbits

B ( ) 안에서 알맞은 것을 고르세요.

1 There (is / are) a cup. 컵 하나가 있다.

2 There (is / are) chairs in the room. 방 안에 의자들이 있다.

3 There (was / were) cookies in a bowl. 그릇 안에 쿠키들이 있었다.

4 There (was / were) a doll in the box. 상자 안에 인형이 하나 있었다.

5 There (is / are) a cushion on the sofa. 소파 위에 쿠션 하나가 있다.

6 There (is / are) many people on the street. 거리에 사람들이 많이 있다.

7 There (was / were) a mirror on the wall. 벽에 거울이 하나 있었다.

「There + be동사」의 부정문과 의문문

● 「There + be동사」의 부정문은 뒤에 not을 써서 나타내며 '~가 없다'라는 뜻이에요.

There is not a mall in this city. 이 도시에는 쇼핑몰이 없다.
There are not any toys here. 여기 장난감이 하나도 없다.
There was not water in the cup. 컵 안에 물이 없었다.
There were not houses on the hill. 언덕 위에 집들이 없었다.

> **Tip** 「There + be동사」의 부정문은 다음과 같이 줄여 쓸 수 있어요.
>
> There is not → There **isn't**　　There are not → There **aren't**
> There was not → There **wasn't**　　There were not → There **weren't**
> There **aren't** horses on this farm.　이 농장에는 말들이 없다.

● 「There + be동사」의 의문문은 「be동사 + there ~?」로 쓰며 '~가 있니?'라는 뜻이에요.

Is there oil in the cupboard? 찬장에 기름이 있니?
Are there any lions in the zoo? 동물원에 사자들이 있니?
Was there a vase on the table? 탁자 위에 꽃병이 있었니?

● 의문문에 대한 긍정 대답은 「Yes, there + be동사.」, 부정 대답은 「No, there + be동사 + not.」의 형태예요.

A: **Are there** many flowers in the garden? 정원에 많은 꽃들이 있니?
B: **Yes, there are.** 응, 있어.

A: **Was there** juice in the cup? 컵 안에 주스가 있었니?
B: **No, there wasn't.** 아니, 없었어.

A 부정문으로 바꿀 때 not이 들어갈 위치를 고르세요.

1 There ⓐ is ⓑ a laptop ⓒ on the desk.　책상 위에 노트북 컴퓨터가 있다.

2 There ⓐ were ⓑ many singers ⓒ at the festival.　그 축제에 많은 가수들이 있었다.

3 There ⓐ are ⓑ grapes ⓒ in the kitchen.　부엌에 포도들이 있다.

4 There was ⓐ a ⓑ cup ⓒ on the table.　탁자 위에 컵이 있었다.

5 There is ⓐ a ⓑ bank ⓒ around here.　여기 근처에 은행이 있다.

6 There ⓐ was ⓑ fruit juice ⓒ in the cup.　컵 안에 과일 주스가 있었다.

7 There ⓐ were ⓑ pigs ⓒ on the farm.　농장에 돼지들이 있었다.

B 빈칸에 들어갈 말로 알맞은 것을 고르세요.

1 _________ there a school here before?　ⓐ Is　ⓑ Was
이곳에 전에 학교가 있었니?

2 _________ there students in the classroom?　ⓐ Is　ⓑ Are
교실에 학생들이 있니?

3 _________ there stars in the sky last night?　ⓐ Are　ⓑ Were
어젯밤에 하늘에 별들이 있었니?

4 _________ there a good restaurant near here?　ⓐ Is　ⓑ Are
여기 근처에 좋은 식당이 있니?

5 _________ there scissors on the desk?　ⓐ Is　ⓑ Are
책상 위에 가위가 있니?

6 _________ there a museum in the town?　ⓐ Was　ⓑ Were
그 도시에는 박물관이 있었니?

「There + be동사」의 현재형과 과거형의 쓰임을 익혀요.

A There is 또는 There are 다음에 쓸 수 있는 말을 분류하여 쓰세요.

> 보기
>
> juice   bread   children   a rainbow   trees
> a bird   oranges   a fish   flowers   mirrors

1 There is

juice

2 There are

B There was 또는 There were 중 알맞은 것을 빈칸에 쓰세요.

1 _There was_ a baseball team in this school.   이 학교에는 야구팀이 있었다.

2 _________________ many people on the subway.   지하철에 많은 사람들이 있었다.

3 _________________ a tall tree on the hill.   언덕 위에 큰 나무가 한 그루 있었다.

4 _________________ a painting on the wall.   벽에 그림이 하나 있었다.

5 _________________ two birds in the cage.   새장 안에 새 두 마리가 있었다.

6 _________________ butter in the refrigerator.   냉장고 안에 버터가 있었다.

7 _________________ many customers at the mall.   쇼핑몰에 많은 고객들이 있었다.

8 _________________ many tourists at the palace.   궁전에 많은 관광객들이 있었다.

LET'S PRACTICE 2

「There + be동사」의 부정문과 의문문의 형태를 익혀요.

A 보기 에서 알맞은 말을 골라 쓰세요. (중복 사용 가능)

| 보기 | There isn't | There aren't | There wasn't | There weren't |

1 _There weren't_ any new buildings last year. 작년에 새 건물들이 전혀 없었다.

2 _________________ a concert yesterday. 어제 콘서트가 없었다.

3 _________________ an eraser in the drawer now. 지금은 서랍 안에 지우개가 없다.

4 _________________ a rainbow in the sky now. 지금은 하늘에 무지개가 없다.

5 _________________ many animals in the zoo yesterday.
어제 동물원에는 동물들이 많이 없었다.

6 _________________ any children in the playground right now.
지금 놀이터에 아이들이 전혀 없다.

B 밑줄 친 부분이 맞으면 ○, 틀리면 X 표시하세요.

1 Are there turtles on the beach? ➞ _____○_____
해변에 거북이들이 있니?

2 Are there ice in the cup? ➞ _________
컵 안에 얼음이 있니?

3 There not was any juice in the refrigerator. ➞ _________
냉장고 안에 주스가 전혀 없었다.

4 There weren't any pens in the pencil case. ➞ _________
필통 안에 펜들이 전혀 없었다.

5 Was there dolphins in the zoo? ➞ _________
동물원에 돌고래들이 있었니?

A 밑줄 친 부분을 바르게 고쳐 쓰세요. (부정문은 축약형으로 쓰세요.)

1 There <u>are</u> a school near here. → _______There is_______
여기 근처에 학교가 하나 있다.

2 There <u>weren't</u> a theater in my town. → ___________________
나의 마을에는 극장이 없었다.

3 <u>Are there</u> oil in the pan? → ___________________
팬에 기름이 있니?

4 There <u>are</u> kids on the beach yesterday morning. → ___________________
어제 아침에 바닷가에 아이들이 있었다.

5 There <u>is</u> not many trees on this mountain. → ___________________
이 산에는 나무들이 많이 없다.

6 There <u>wasn't</u> any muffins in the basket. → ___________________
바구니 안에는 머핀들이 전혀 없었다.

7 <u>Is there</u> many benches in the park? → ___________________
공원에 벤치가 많이 있니?

8 There <u>aren't</u> any hope. → ___________________
희망이 전혀 없다.

9 There <u>isn't</u> many people in the park. → ___________________
공원에는 사람들이 많이 없다.

10 <u>Was there</u> many holidays last year? → ___________________
작년에는 휴일들이 많았니?

B 다음 문장을 주어진 지시대로 바꿔 쓸 때 빈칸에 알맞은 말을 쓰세요.

1 There are two singers on the stage. (과거형) 무대 위에 두 명의 가수가 있다.

➡ _____There_____ _____were_____ two singers on the stage.

2 There were cows on the farm. (의문문) 농장에는 소들이 있었다.

➡ ___________ ___________ cows on the farm?

3 There are flowers on the cake. (부정문) 케이크 위에 꽃들이 있다.

➡ ___________ ___________ any flowers on the cake.

4 There is a bird on the roof. (의문문) 지붕 위에 새가 있다.

➡ ___________ ___________ a bird on the roof?

5 There were toys on the floor. (현재형) 바닥에 장난감들이 있었다.

➡ ___________ ___________ toys on the floor.

6 There is some bread on the plate. (과거형) 접시에 약간의 빵이 있다.

➡ ___________ ___________ some bread on the plate.

7 There were shoes under the sofa. (부정문) 소파 아래에 신발이 있었다.

➡ ___________ ___________ any shoes under the sofa.

8 There are many fish in this pond. (의문문) 이 연못에는 많은 물고기들이 있다.

➡ ___________ ___________ many fish in this pond?

9 There is an Italian restaurant downtown. (부정문) 시내에 이탈리아 식당이 있다.

➡ ___________ ___________ an Italian restaurant downtown.

10 There was a cup of coffee on the table. (현재형) 탁자 위에 커피 한 잔이 있었다.

➡ ___________ ___________ a cup of coffee on the table.

A 빈칸에 알맞은 말을 넣어 대화를 완성하세요.

1 A: Was there a bank across the street? 길 건너편에 은행이 있었니?

  B: No, ____there____ ____wasn't____ . 아니, 없었어.

2 A: Is there a museum in this city? 이 도시에는 박물관이 있니?

  B: ____________, ____________ is. 응, 있어.

3 A: Is there a subway station near here? 여기 근처에 지하철역이 있니?

  B: No, ____________ ____________. 아니, 없어.

4 A: ____________ ____________ apple trees in the garden?

  정원에 사과 나무들이 있니?

  B: Yes, there are. 응, 있어.

5 A: Were there bees on the flowers? 꽃들 위에 벌들이 있었니?

  B: No, ____________ ____________. 아니, 없었어.

6 A: Are there pants in the closet? 옷장 안에 바지가 있니?

  B: No, ____________ ____________. 아니, 없어.

7 A: ____________ ____________ dust on the desk? 책상 위에 먼지가 있었니?

  B: Yes, there was. 응, 있었어.

8 A: Were there many festivals last year? 작년에 많은 축제들이 있었니?

  B: No, ____________ ____________. 아니, 없었어.

9 A: Are there cups in the cupboard? 찬장 안에 컵들이 있니?

  B: Yes, ____________ ____________. 응, 있어.

10 A: Was there orange juice in the cup? 컵 안에 오렌지주스가 있었니?

  B: Yes, ____________ ____________. 응, 있었어.

B 사진을 보고 주어진 말을 이용하여 빈칸에 알맞은 말을 쓰세요.

1 ___There___ ___are___ ___oranges___ in the basket. (oranges)
바구니 안에 오렌지들이 있다.

2 There ___________ ___________ ___________ on the sofa. (a puppy)
소파 위에는 강아지가 없다.

3 ___________ ___________ any ___________ on the tray. (grapes)
쟁반 위에는 포도가 전혀 없다.

4 A: ___________ ___________ ___________ on the roof? (leaves) 지붕 위에 나뭇잎들이 있니?
B: Yes, there are. 응, 있어.

5 ___________ ___________ ___________ on this mountain before. (houses)
전에 이 산에는 집들이 있었다.

6 ___________ ___________ ___________ on the plate. (pasta)
접시 위에 파스타가 있다.

STEP UP 3

A 우리말과 같은 뜻이 되도록 주어진 말을 이용하여 빈칸에 알맞은 말을 쓰세요.

1 이곳에는 신발이 전혀 없다. (shoes)

➡ __There__ __aren't__ any __shoes__ here.

2 상자 안에 고양이가 한 마리 있다. (a cat)

➡ ______ ______ ______ ______ in the box.

3 책상 위에는 식물이 없었다. (a plant)

➡ ______ ______ ______ ______ on the desk.

4 정원에 많은 곤충들이 있니? (many insects)

➡ ______ ______ ______ ______ in the garden?

5 농장에는 닭들이 있었다. (chickens)

➡ ______ ______ ______ on the farm.

6 내 지갑 속에는 돈이 전혀 없다. (money)

➡ ______ ______ any ______ in my wallet.

7 하늘에 구름들이 있다. (clouds)

➡ ______ ______ ______ in the sky.

8 케이크 위에 양초들이 있었니? (candles)

➡ ______ ______ ______ on the cake?

9 내 가방 안에는 공책이 없었다. (a notebook)

➡ ______ ______ ______ ______ in my bag.

10 지붕 위에 사다리가 있었니? (a ladder)

➡ ______ ______ ______ ______ on the roof?

ⓑ 우리말과 같은 뜻이 되도록 주어진 말을 바르게 배열하세요.

1 하늘에 두 개의 무지개가 있다. (are / two rainbows / there)

→ ____________There are two rainbows____________ in the sky.

2 우리 안에 햄스터 한 마리가 있었다. (was / there / a hamster)

→ ________________________________ in the cage.

3 그 가게에는 손님들이 전혀 없었다. (there / any customers / weren't)

→ ________________________________ in the store.

4 어항에는 물고기들이 전혀 없다. (any fish / there / aren't)

→ ________________________________ in the fishbowl.

5 식탁 위에 두 개의 접시가 있었다. (there / two dishes / were)

→ ________________________________ on the table.

6 바닥에 카펫이 있다. (a carpet / there / is)

→ ________________________________ on the floor.

7 냉장고 안에 물이 전혀 없었다. (there / any water / wasn't)

→ ________________________________ in the refrigerator.

8 찬장 안에 차가 있니? (is / tea / there)

→ ________________________________ in the cupboard?

9 여기 주변에 오래된 건물들이 있니? (there / old buildings / are)

→ ________________________________ around here?

10 옷장 안에 많은 옷들이 있었니? (were / many clothes / there)

→ ________________________________ in the closet?

STEP UP 4

A 다음 문장을 주어진 지시대로 바꿔 쓰세요. (부정문은 축약형으로 쓰세요.)

1 There is a movie poster on the wall. (의문문)　벽에 영화 포스터가 있다.

→ _Is there a movie poster on the wall?_

2 There are many books on the desk. (부정문)　책상 위에 많은 책들이 있다.

→ ___________________

3 There is yogurt in the bowl. (과거형)　그릇 안에 요거트가 있다.

→ ___________________

4 There is a closet in the room. (부정문)　방안에 옷장이 있다.

→ ___________________

5 There are tomatoes in the refrigerator. (과거형)　냉장고 안에 토마토들이 있다.

→ ___________________

6 There were many sheep on the hill. (부정문)　언덕 위에 많은 양들이 있었다.

→ ___________________

7 There was a wallet in this bag. (의문문)　이 가방 안에 지갑이 하나 있었다.

→ ___________________

8 There are children at the amusement park. (의문문)　놀이공원에 아이들이 있다.

→ ___________________

9 There was a trash can on the beach. (부정문)　해변에 쓰레기통이 하나 있었다.

→ ___________________

10 There were elephants in the zoo. (의문문)　동물원에 코끼리들이 있었다.

→ ___________________

B 밑줄 친 부분을 바르게 고쳐 문장을 다시 쓰세요.

1 There <u>are</u> a French restaurant downtown.   시내에 프랑스 식당이 있다.

→ There is a French restaurant downtown.

2 <u>There is</u> a baseball stadium in this city?   이 도시에는 야구 경기장이 있니?

→

3 <u>Was there</u> many bikes on the street?   거리에 자전거들이 많이 있었니?

→

4 <u>There was</u> many tourists on the island.   그 섬에는 많은 관광객들이 있었다.

→

5 <u>Were there</u> a basketball team in this school?   이 학교에는 농구팀이 있었니?

→

6 <u>There were</u> a smartphone under the sofa.   소파 아래에 스마트폰이 있었다.

→

7 <u>There wasn't</u> any monkeys in the zoo.   동물원에 원숭이들이 전혀 없었다.

→

8 <u>There is</u> toys in my room.   내 방에 장난감들이 있다.

→

9 <u>There weren't</u> a department store in my town.   나의 마을에는 백화점이 없었다.

→

10 <u>There isn't</u> any toothbrushes in the bathroom.   화장실에 칫솔들이 전혀 없다.

→

LEVEL UP

A 우리말과 같은 뜻이 되도록 빈칸에 알맞은 말을 쓰세요.

1 ____There____ ____were____ ____toys____ on the floor.
바닥에 장난감들이 있었다.

2 ____________ ____________ any ____________ in the playground right now.
지금 놀이터에 아이들이 전혀 없다.

3 A: Were there dolphins in the zoo?
동물원에 돌고래들이 있었니?

B: Yes, ____________ ____________. 응, 있었어.

4 ____________ ____________ a ____________ ____________ on the beach.
해변에 쓰레기통이 없었다.

5 ____________ ____________ a ____________ ____________ in this city?
이 도시에는 야구 경기장이 있니?

6 ____________ ____________ ____________ ____________ under the sofa.
소파 아래에 스마트폰이 있었다.

B 우리말과 같은 뜻이 되도록 빈칸에 알맞은 말을 쓰세요.

1 __________Are__________ __________there__________ __________turtles__________ on the beach?
해변에 거북이들이 있니?

2 __________ __________ __________ __________ in the box.
상자 안에 인형이 하나 있었다.

3 __________ __________ any __________ in the zoo.
동물원에 원숭이들이 전혀 없었다.

4 __________ __________ __________ in the room.
방 안에 의자들이 있다.

5 __________ __________ __________ last year?
작년에는 휴일들이 많았니?

6 __________ __________ a __________ in the sky now.
지금은 하늘에 무지개가 없다.

7 __________ __________ any __________ in the refrigerator.
냉장고 안에 주스가 전혀 없었다.

8 __________ __________ __________ in the pan?
팬에 기름이 있니?

9 __________ __________ __________ on the farm.
농장에는 소들이 있었다.

10 __________ __________ a __________ on the roof.
지붕 위에 새가 있다.

11 __________ __________ any __________ here.
이곳에는 신발이 전혀 없다.

12 __________ __________ a __________ here before?
이곳에 전에 학교가 있었니?

REVIEW TEST

[1~3] 사진을 보고 ( ) 안에서 알맞은 것을 고르세요.

1

There (is / are) coffee in the cup.

2

There (is / are) flowers in the vase.

3

There (was / were) a polar bear in the snow.

4 빈칸에 들어갈 알맞은 말을 고르세요.

_______________ bananas on the table.

① There is ② There was ③ There isn't ④ There were

5 질문에 대한 대답으로 알맞은 것을 고르세요.

Is there a bookstore near here?

① Yes, it is. ② Yes, there are.

③ No, there isn't. ④ No, there aren't.

6 빈칸에 공통으로 알맞은 말을 고르세요.

> · There _____________ a bakery on the corner before.
> · _____________ there any water in the glass?

① is[Is]　　　② are[Are]　　　③ was[Was]　　　④ were[Were]

7 빈칸에 들어갈 말이 나머지와 <u>다른</u> 것을 고르세요.

① There _________ some bread in the kitchen.

② _________ there an airplane in the sky now?

③ There _________ a clock on the wall.

④ There _________ many parks in this city.

8 밑줄 친 부분이 <u>어색한</u> 것을 고르세요.

① There <u>is</u> a big farm in the town.

② There <u>were</u> many students in the playground.

③ There <u>wasn't</u> any chairs in the office.

④ There <u>is</u> some milk in the refrigerator.

9 빈칸에 들어갈 수 <u>없는</u> 말을 고르세요.

> There is ______________ in the bowl.

① an egg ② some rice ③ cherries ④ a tomato

10 빈칸에 들어갈 말이 바르게 짝지어진 것을 고르세요.

> · There ______________ a piece of cake on the table.
> · ______________ there many tourists in this city before?

① is – Are ② is – Were ③ are – Are ④ are – Were

11 어법상 <u>틀린</u> 문장을 고르세요.

① There is a beautiful palace before.

② There wasn't any trash on the street.

③ Are there many cars on the road?

④ There is a bed in my room.

12 우리말을 영어로 바르게 옮긴 것을 고르세요.

> 내 지갑에는 돈이 하나도 없었다.

① There isn't any money in my wallet.

② There wasn't any money in my wallet.

③ There aren't any money in my wallet.

④ There weren't any money in my wallet.

서술형
13 우리말과 같은 뜻이 되도록 주어진 말을 바르게 배열하세요.

> 나무에 많은 새들이 있었다.
>
> (there / many birds / in the tree / were / .)

➜ ____

서술형
14 보기 와 같은 규칙으로 다음 문장을 완성하세요.

> 보기 A blanket is on the bed.
> → Is there a blanket on the bed?

Tigers were in the zoo.

➜ ____

서술형
15 다음 그림을 보고 질문에 답하세요. (부정문은 축약형으로 쓰세요.)

A: Are there four ducks on the pond?

B: ___________________________________

A: Is there a boy near the pond?

B: ___________________________________

A: Are there two frogs on the rocks?

B: ___________________________________

실전 Test 02회

[1~2] 빈칸에 들어갈 알맞은 말을 고르세요.

1
> There __________ some cheese on the dish.

① is   ② are
③ aren't   ④ were

2
> My brother __________ sick last night.

① is   ② was
③ isn't   ④ weren't

3 질문에 대한 대답으로 알맞은 것을 고르세요.

> Were you at the department store an hour ago?

① Yes, I am.   ② No, we wasn't.
③ Yes, we were.   ④ No, I'm not.

4 우리말을 영어로 바르게 옮긴 것을 고르세요.

> 벽에 시계가 하나 있었다.

① There is a clock on the wall.
② There was a clock on the wall.
③ There are a clock on the wall.
④ There were a clock on the wall.

[5~6] 빈칸에 들어갈 수 <u>없는</u> 말을 고르세요.

5
> There aren't __________ on the road.

① any cars   ② many people
③ any trees   ④ a bike

6
> The orange __________ sweet.

① was   ② wasn't
③ is   ④ were

7 빈칸에 공통으로 알맞은 말을 고르세요.

> • ___________ there many apples on the tree last year?
> • They ___________ at the temple last Sunday.

① Is[is] ② Are[are]

③ Was[was] ④ Were[were]

[8~9] 밑줄 친 부분이 어색한 것을 고르세요.

8 ① There <u>was</u> a piece of cake on the plate.

② There <u>were</u> two beds in the bedroom before.

③ There <u>is</u> some clothes in the closet.

④ There <u>is</u> a kite in the sky.

9 ① I <u>wasn't</u> late for school this morning.

② <u>Was</u> the restaurant open yesterday?

③ They <u>were</u> at the gym then.

④ The tomato soup <u>weren't</u> salty.

[10~11] 빈칸에 들어갈 말이 나머지와 <u>다른</u> 것을 고르세요.

10 ① _______ there many flowers in the garden now?

② There _______ cows and pigs on the farm now.

③ _______ there milk in the cup?

④ There _______ not any fruits in the basket now.

11 ① He _______ not busy last week.

② The kids _______ in the park ten minutes ago.

③ _______ Danny a violinist in 2015?

④ The wind _______ very strong yesterday.

12 밑줄 친 부분의 의미가 나머지와 <u>다른</u> 것을 고르세요.

① Peter <u>was</u> my coworker.

② Mr. Wilson <u>was</u> a teacher.

③ My parents <u>were</u> in the living room.

④ She <u>was</u> a tennis player before.

13

> · __________ there penguins in the zoo?
> · There __________ a mirror in the room.

① Are – aren't　② Is – aren't

③ Are – isn't　④ Is – isn't

14

> A: __________ it cold last winter?
> B: No, it __________.

① Is – wasn't　② Was – wasn't

③ Is – weren't　④ Was – weren't

15 밑줄 친 부분을 바르게 고친 것을 고르세요.

> · There aren't a café around here before.
> · Are there some olive oil in the salad?

① isn't – Is　② isn't – Were

③ wasn't – Were　④ wasn't – Is

[16~17] 어법상 틀린 문장을 고르세요.

16 ① These books was popular.

② He was friendly to his customers.

③ The dishes weren't clean.

④ Were you tired last night?

17 ① Are there hospitals near the school?

② There are famous models on the stage.

③ There wasn't any ice in the refrigerator.

④ There not were any cups in the shop.

18 대화가 어색한 것을 고르세요.

① A: Was the movie scary?
B: No, it wasn't.

② A: Were the cookies tasty?
B: Yes, it was.

③ A: Was he an actor before?
B: Yes, he was.

④ A: Were the kids excited?
B: No, they weren't.

19 다음 문장을 주어진 지시대로 바꿔 쓰세요.

> (1) The game was really exciting at that time. (의문문)

→ ______________________________

____

> (2) There is a lamp on the desk.
> (부정문)

→ ______________________________

____

20 우리말과 같은 뜻이 되도록 주어진 말을 바르게 배열하세요.

> 쇼핑몰에 많은 사람들이 있었니?
> (many people / there / at the mall / were / ?)

→ ______________________________

____

21 어법상 <u>틀린</u> 부분을 찾아 바르게 고쳐 쓰세요.

> The pants was big for me last year.

______________ → ______________

22 다음 그림을 보고 「There + be동사」를 빈칸에 알맞은 형태로 쓰세요.

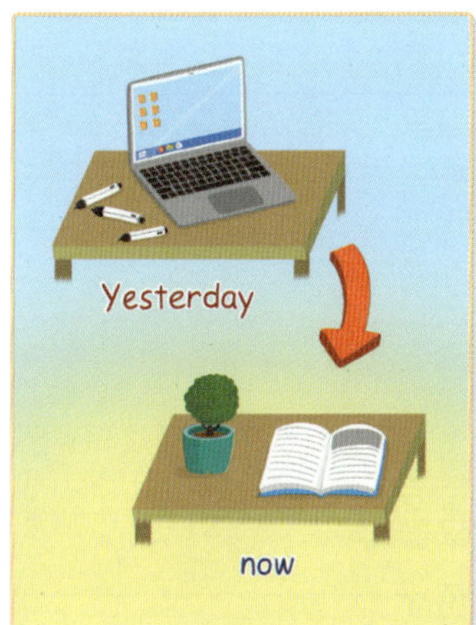

> (1) __________ __________ a laptop on the desk yesterday.
> (2) __________ __________ a plant on the desk yesterday.
> (3) __________ __________ a book on the desk now.
> (4) __________ __________ any pens on the desk now.

지은이

NE능률 영어교육연구소

NE능률 영어교육연구소는 혁신적이며 효율적인 영어 교재를 개발하고
영어 학습의 질을 한 단계 높이고자 노력하는 NE능률의 연구조직입니다.

초등 Grammar Inside 〈2권〉

펴 낸 이	이정진
펴 낸 곳	서울특별시 마포구 월드컵북로 396(상암동) 누리꿈스퀘어 비즈니스타워 10층
	㈜NE능률 (우편번호 03925)
펴 낸 날	2022년 1월 5일 초판 제1쇄 발행
	2025년 12월 15일 제14쇄
전 화	02 2014 7114
팩 스	02 3142 0356
홈 페 이 지	www.neungyule.com
등 록 번 호	제1-68호
I S B N	979-11-253-3711-9 63740
정 가	13,000원

NE 능률

고객센터

교재 내용 문의 : contact.nebooks.co.kr (별도의 가입 절차 없이 작성 가능)

제품 구매, 교환, 불량, 반품 문의 : 02-2014-7114

☎ 전화문의는 본사 업무시간 중에만 가능합니다.

[01~02] 동사원형과 3인칭 단수형이 잘못 짝지어진 것을 고르세요.

01
① pass – passes   ② do – does
③ fly – flies   ④ watch – watches
⑤ enjoy – enjoies

02
① hurry – hurries   ② brush – brushs
③ play – plays   ④ love – loves
⑤ fix – fixes

[03~04] 빈칸에 들어갈 알맞은 말을 고르세요.

03
There _________ some plants in the living room before.

① be   ② is
③ are   ④ was
⑤ were

04
My sister _________ watch horror movies.

① isn't   ② don't
③ doesn't   ④ am
⑤ aren't

05 질문에 대한 대답으로 알맞은 것을 고르세요.

Does he need a new shirt?

① Yes, he do.   ② No, he don't.
③ No, he doesn't.   ④ Yes, he is.
⑤ No, he isn't.

[06~07] 빈칸에 들어갈 수 없는 말을 고르세요.

06
She _________ early in the morning.

① gets up   ② studies
③ exercise   ④ swims
⑤ sings

07
Is there _________ in the refrigerator?

① milk   ② some cheese
③ yogurt   ④ eggs
⑤ cold water

08 빈칸에 was[Was]가 들어갈 수 없는 문장을 고르세요.

① Steve _______ at the library an hour ago.
② Mark and I _______ not friends three years ago.
③ It _______ clear and sunny yesterday.
④ _______ the singer popular before?
⑤ Your bag _______ on the chair before.

[09~10] 빈칸에 들어갈 말이 바르게 짝지어진 것을 고르세요.

09
• She doesn't _________ coffee in the evening.
• _________ they raise pets?

① drink – Does   ② drink – Do
③ drinks – Do   ④ drinks – Does
⑤ drinkes – Do

10
• We _______ classmates last year.
• _______ there a closet in your room before?

① are – Is   ② are – Was
③ was – Were   ④ were – Is
⑤ were – Was

11 ① They <u>doesn't</u> like Chinese food.
② <u>Does</u> he teach math?
③ Some people <u>don't</u> eat meat.
④ <u>Do</u> you take a ballet lesson every day?
⑤ My dog <u>doesn't</u> bark.

12 ① <u>Was</u> your daughter sick yesterday?
② My parents <u>were</u> at home last night.
③ They <u>is</u> French.
④ <u>Was</u> the ticket expensive?
⑤ Taylor <u>wasn't</u> tall before.

13 대화가 어색한 것을 고르세요.

① A: Was the book popular?
　B: Yes, it was.
② A: Were there many people at the restaurant?
　B: Yes, they were.
③ A: Were you a nurse before?
　B: No, I wasn't.
④ A: Was it cold last week?
　B: No, it wasn't.
⑤ A: Were your friends at the gym?
　B: Yes, they were.

14 우리말을 영어로 바르게 옮긴 것을 고르세요.

그 가게는 커피를 팔지 않는다.

① The store don't sell coffee.
② The store don't sells coffee.
③ The store doesn't sells coffee.
④ The store doesn't sell coffee.
⑤ The store don't selles coffee.

15 어법상 틀린 문장을 고르세요.

① Frogs sleep in the winter.
② The musical finishes at 9:00 p.m.
③ My grandfather miss his hometown.
④ They walk to school.
⑤ Jessica goes to the café every day.

16 우리말과 같은 뜻이 되도록 빈칸에 알맞은 말을 쓰세요.

우리는 한 시간 전에 극장에 있지 않았다. 우리는 박물관에 있었다.

→ We ________________ at the theater an hour

　ago. We ________________ at the museum.

[17~18] 어법상 틀린 부분을 찾아 바르게 고쳐 쓰세요.

17 Rona drys her hair every day.

________________ → ________________

18 A: Does Peter have blond hair?
　　B: Yes, he has.

________________ → ________________

[19~20] 우리말과 같은 뜻이 되도록 주어진 말을 바르게 배열하세요.

19 거리에 나무들이 많았니?
(many trees / were / on the street / there / ?)

→ ________________

20 그녀는 슬픈 음악을 좋아하지 않는다.
(not / sad music / she / like / does / .)

→ ________________

01 동사원형과 3인칭 단수형이 바르게 짝지어진 것을 고르세요.

① try – trys ② go – gos
③ cry – cries ④ wash – washs
⑤ read – reades

[02~03] 빈칸에 들어갈 알맞은 말을 고르세요.

02

It __________ my favorite song before.

① is ② are
③ am ④ was
⑤ were

03

__________ there a bird in the sky now?

① Am ② Is
③ Are ④ Was
⑤ Were

[04~05] 빈칸에 들어갈 수 <u>없는</u> 말을 고르세요.

04

__________ speaks French very well.

① She ② You
③ Mina ④ My uncle
⑤ The woman

05

__________ don't wear glasses.

① I ② They
③ My parents ④ The kids
⑤ Jake

[06~07] 질문에 대한 대답으로 알맞은 것을 고르세요.

06

Are there roses in the garden?

① Yes, it is. ② No, there wasn't.
③ Yes, there are. ④ No, there isn't.
⑤ Yes, there were.

07

Does he play basketball after school?

① Yes, he is. ② Yes, he does.
③ No, he isn't. ④ No, he does.
⑤ Yes, he was.

08 빈칸에 were[Were]가 들어갈 수 <u>없는</u> 문장을 고르세요.

① They ________ soccer players before.
② The pizza ________ not salty.
③ ________ the birds on the roof?
④ ________ you late for the class?
⑤ The shoes ________ not small for me.

09 어법상 <u>틀린</u> 문장을 고르세요.

① The medicine doesn't taste bitter.
② Do monkeys like bananas?
③ Does your sister play hockey?
④ She doesn't needs a new laptop.
⑤ Do you cook well?

10 우리말을 영어로 바르게 옮긴 것을 고르세요.

바구니 안에는 달걀들이 전혀 없었다.

① There is not any eggs in the basket.
② There are not any egg in the basket.
③ There was not any eggs in the basket.
④ There were not any eggs in the basket.
⑤ There weren't any egg in the basket.

[11~12] 빈칸에 들어갈 말이 바르게 짝지어진 것을 고르세요.

11

A: _______ there coffee in the cup?
B: Yes, _______.

① Is – there are　　② Are – there was
③ Was – there was　　④ Were – there were
⑤ Was – there wasn't

12

• We _______ have a car.
• Patrick doesn't _______ TV.

① don't – watch　　② don't – watchs
③ don't – watches　　④ doesn't – watches
⑤ doesn't – watchs

[13~14] 밑줄 친 부분이 어색한 것을 고르세요.

13 ① <u>Is</u> there ice in the refrigerator now?
② There <u>wasn't</u> a clock on the wall before.
③ There <u>is</u> an ice rink in this town.
④ There <u>aren't</u> bread on the plate.
⑤ <u>Were</u> there children in the park yesterday?

14 ① I <u>take</u> a shower every evening.
② My dad <u>washes</u> the dishes after dinner.
③ A kite <u>flys</u> high in the sky.
④ We <u>like</u> fast food.
⑤ It <u>rains</u> a lot in the spring.

15 대화가 어색한 것을 고르세요.

① A: Does the train leave at 12:30?
　 B: Yes, he does.
② A: Do Amy and Josh like hamburgers?
　 B: No, they don't.
③ A: Does Kelly walk her dog every day?
　 B: Yes, she does.
④ A: Does he play online games a lot?
　 B: Yes, he does.
⑤ A: Do you want some more cake?
　 B: No, I don't.

[16~17] 다음 문장을 주어진 지시대로 바꿔 쓰세요. (부정문은 축약형으로 쓰세요.)

16

My cat has a long tail. (부정문)

→ _______________________________________

17

There were many goats on the farm. (의문문)

→ _______________________________________

18 우리말과 같은 뜻이 되도록 주어진 말을 바르게 배열하세요.

그녀는 내 이름을 안다.
(knows / my name / she / .)

→ _______________________________________

19 우리말과 같은 뜻이 되도록 빈칸에 알맞은 말을 쓰세요.

근처에 카페가 하나 있다.

→ ______________ ______________ a café nearby.

20 어법상 틀린 부분을 찾아 바르게 고쳐 쓰세요.

My son don't enjoy swimming.

______________ → ______________

초등 Grammar Inside

Answer Key

2

초등 Grammar Inside

Student Book
Answer Key

2

Chapter 01 일반동사

Unit 01 일반동사의 종류

CHECK UP p.9

A know, listen, drink, clean, play, jump, make, hit, walk, read, live

B 1. V 2. X 3. V 4. X 5. V 6. V

Unit 02 일반동사의 현재형

CHECK UP p.11

A 1. run, 일반적 사실 2. need, 현재의 상태
3. love, 현재의 상태 4. wash, 반복되는 습관
5. have, 일반적 사실

해석 1 치타들은 매우 빠르게 달린다.
2 나는 사전이 필요하다.
3 그들은 버터 쿠키를 무척 좋아한다.
4 나는 내 손을 자주 씻는다.
5 개미들은 여섯 개의 다리를 가지고 있다.

B 1. walk 2. taste 3. sing 4. swims

LET'S PRACTICE 1 p.12

A 1. understand 2. want 3. Draw
4. speak 5. do 6. feel

B 1. play, drink, run, make, talk
2. know, hate, feel, love, think

LET'S PRACTICE 2 p.13

A 1. have 2. brush 3. is 4. eat
5. are 6. shines

B 1. play 2. looks 3. helps 4. wear
5. hate 6. use

STEP UP 1 p.14

A 1. read 2. enjoy 3. go 4. get up
5. learn 6. come 7. run 8. use
9. take 10. love 11. wear

B 1. sleep 2. like 3. grows 4. know
5. arrives 6. dance 7. sounds 8. work
9. write 10. play 11. ride 12. hates

STEP UP 2 p.16

A 1. have 2. reads 3. eat 4. fly
5. looks 6. sleeps

B 1. dry 2. meets 3. help 4. answers
5. shine 6. feel 7. needs 8. bake
9. likes 10. drive 11. hates

STEP UP 3 p.18

A 1. clean, cleans 2. love, loves
3. wants, want 4. save, saves
5. buys, buy 6. smells, smell
7. pull, pulls 8. visit, visits

B 1. I understand 2. She learns
3. We go 4. Kate writes
5. They eat 6. Harry plays
7. I miss 8. live in
9. I feel 10. He takes

STEP UP 4 p.20

A 1. wants a smartphone
2. cook dinner every day
3. works well
4. drink tea after breakfast
5. runs really slowly
6. eat pizza on Saturdays
7. stays home at night
8. play soccer every weekend
9. spend too much money
10. shouts a lot

B 1. Dora speaks Spanish.
2. We want a bowl of salad.
3. I borrow books from the library.
4. This hamburger tastes really good.
5. It looks like an interesting video.
6. I clean the bathroom on Wednesdays.

7. Bella and Larry work at the school.
8. The loud sound comes from there.
9. The woman sings a song every night.
10. Pandas eat bamboo.

LEVEL UP p.22

A
1. buys, mall
2. Those dancers dance
3. Snow comes
4. She meets, Tuesdays
5. I ride, bike[bicycle]
6. They play hockey

B
1. want some butter　　2. swims very well
3. hates coffee　　4. You use, water
5. looks, dirty　　6. She needs, paper
7. drinks tea after　　8. tree grows, fast
9. Bakers bake bread　10. plays with robots
11. save many lives　12. cleans, floor alone

Unit 03 　일반동사의 3인칭 단수형 (1)

CHECK UP p.25

A　1. ⓐ　2. ⓑ　3. ⓑ　4. ⓐ　5. ⓐ　6. ⓑ

B　1. walk　2. rains　3. open　4. helps

Unit 04 　일반동사의 3인칭 단수형 (2)

CHECK UP p.27

A　1. ⓑ　2. ⓑ　3. ⓑ　4. ⓐ　5. ⓑ　6. ⓐ

B　1. has　2. drives　3. studies　4. does
5. snows　6. scratches

LET'S PRACTICE 1 p.28

A
1. loves, trains, hates
2. swim, sleep, sing, dance

B　1. want　2. reads　3. feel　4. tastes
5. take　6. needs

LET'S PRACTICE 2 p.29

A　1. goes　2. catches　3. cries　4. opens
5. brushes　6. says　7. relaxes

B　1. O　2. X　3. O　4. X　5. O　6. X

STEP UP 1 p.30

A　1. teaches　2. speaks　3. grows　4. live
5. goes　6. has　7. remember
8. washes　9. flies　10. look　11. plays

B　1. misses　2. eats　3. know　4. carries
5. comes　6. touches　7. want　8. likes
9. uses　10. fix

STEP UP 2 p.32

A　1. crosses　2. tastes　3. walk　4. flies
5. swim　6. has

B　1. live　2. have　3. shines　4. studies
5. drives　6. tries　7. forgets　8. rains
9. finishes　10. teaches　11. jumps

STEP UP 3 p.34

A
1. pay, pays　　2. catch, catches
3. feels, feel　　4. does, do
5. try, tries　　6. mixes, mix
7. saves, save　　8. brush, brushes

B
1. crosses the road
2. live in New York
3. tries to be helpful
4. touches the shelf
5. pass the ball very well
6. goes to the market by bus
7. follow you
8. grow some tomatoes
9. has a stomachache
10. fix the roof

STEP UP 4 p.36

A
1. She has two belts.
2. We study Chinese history.
3. Daniel remembers his aunt.
4. My baby cries a lot.

5. My father acts on the stage.
6. They wash their feet in the bathroom.
7. I use chopsticks very well.
8. The machine makes a lot of noise.
9. I miss the cafeteria in my hometown.
10. Bears sleep in the winter.

B 1. studies Spanish
2. drinks a glass of juice
3. shine brightly
4. drives to the mall
5. goes to the bakery
6. eat too much fast food
7. finishes at 11 o'clock
8. sits next to me
9. dries so fast

LEVEL UP p.38

A 1. look cold
2. The glue dries
3. cat scratches, wall
4. washes her hands
5. uses, spoon, fork
6. My father[dad] acts, stage

B 1. goes to, mall
2. walk to school
3. does yoga
4. fixes cars, work
5. tastes like watermelon
6. It rains a lot
7. take photos[pictures] together
8. uncle teaches math
9. know that movie
10. want yellow sneakers
11. dries her hair
12. misses her hometown

Chapter 01 REVIEW TEST p.40

1. run 2. drinks 3. looks 4. ③ 5. ① 6. ④
7. ② 8. ② 9. ③ 10. ① 11. ③ 12. ④
13. lives 14. She teaches Japanese
15. has, takes, studies, listens, goes

1 주어가 복수이므로 run을 쓴다.
2 주어가 3인칭 단수이므로 drinks를 쓴다.
3 주어가 3인칭 단수이므로 looks를 쓴다.

4 ③ is는 be동사이다.
5 ① '자음 + y'로 끝나는 동사의 3인칭 단수형은 y를 i로 바꾸고 -es를 붙여서 만든다. (drys → dries)
6 ④ every day가 쓰여 반복되는 습관을 나타낸다. 빈칸에는 의미상 일반동사인 go가 들어가야 하는데, 주어가 3인칭 단수이므로 goes가 알맞다.
7 ② plays의 주어 자리에는 3인칭 단수가 와야 한다. ①③④ 3인칭 단수, ② 3인칭 복수
8 ② 주어가 2인칭일 때는 일반동사의 동사원형을 써야 한다. (speaks → speak)
9 ③ 주어(The class)가 3인칭 단수이므로 동사도 3인칭 단수형을 써야 한다. (begin → begins)
10 ① 주어(Ms. Jackson)가 3인칭 단수이므로 동사도 3인칭 단수형을 써야 하는데, enjoy의 3인칭 단수형은 enjoys이다. 주어(Rabbits)가 복수이므로 일반동사의 동사원형을 쓴다.
11 ③ 주어(Matt and Katie)가 복수이므로 일반동사의 동사원형을 쓴다. 주어(A spider)가 3인칭 단수이므로 동사도 3인칭 단수형을 써야 한다.
12 ④ 주어(My sister)가 3인칭 단수이므로 동사도 3인칭 단수형을 써야 한다. (go → goes)
13 주어(My cousin)가 3인칭 단수이므로 동사도 3인칭 단수형인 lives를 쓴다.
14 주어가 3인칭 단수이므로 teach에 -es를 붙여 teaches로 쓴다.
15 주어가 3인칭 단수(Jane, She)일 때는 동사도 3인칭 단수형을 써야 한다.

Chapter 02 일반동사의 부정문과 의문문

Unit 01 일반동사의 부정문

CHECK UP p.47

A 1. V 2. V 3. X 4. V 5. X 6. V 7. V

B 1. O 2. X 3. X 4. X 5. O 6. O

Unit 02 일반동사의 의문문

CHECK UP p.49

A 1. ⓐ 2. ⓑ 3. ⓑ 4. ⓐ 5. ⓐ

B 1. No 2. Do 3. doesn't 4. Do, do

A 1. don't 2. doesn't 3. doesn't
     4. exercise 5. bark

B 1. don't[do not]   2. work
     3. does not[doesn't] 4. doesn't[does not]
     5. jump   6. don't[do not]

LET'S PRACTICE 2   p.51

A 1. Do 2. Does 3. Do 4. Do 5. Does
     6. Does 7. Do

B 1. does 2. don't 3. do 4. doesn't

STEP UP 1   p.52

A 1. doesn't have   2. don't like
     3. doesn't wear   4. doesn't enjoy
     5. don't use   6. doesn't remember
     7. doesn't close   8. don't study
     9. doesn't understand 10. don't miss

B 1. Does she   2. Do snakes
     3. Does Nick   4. Do we

C 1. I do   2. she doesn't
     3. they don't   4. he does

STEP UP 2   p.54

A 1. Do, fight   2. don't go
     3. doesn't have   4. Does, get up
     5. Do, need   6. doesn't like
     7. Does, eat   8. don't speak
     9. don't sing   10. Does, sell

B 1. Does, take, does 2. doesn't have
     3. don't want   4. Do, swim, No
     5. Does, watch, Yes 6. don't feel

STEP UP 3   p.56

A 1. doesn't tell   2. doesn't read
     3. don't understand 4. doesn't study
     5. doesn't end   6. don't use
     7. don't exercise   8. doesn't sell
     9. doesn't play   10. don't know

B 1. Does, rain, it does

2. Do, eat, they don't
3. Do, look, they don't
4. Does, help, she does
5. Does, work, he doesn't
6. Does, sound, it does
7. Do, hate, they don't
8. Does, need, he does

STEP UP 4   p.58

A 1. Do bears sleep all winter?
     2. The train doesn't leave at 4:30 a.m.
     3. Does this blanket feel soft?
     4. I don't enjoy skating.
     5. He doesn't like sad movies.
     6. Does Britney go to bed early?
     7. Those girls don't live in Kenya.
     8. Do they go to the dentist?
     9. Annie doesn't dance very well.
    10. Do my socks look clean?

B 1. Does, play tennis, she does
     2. Does, No, she doesn't
     3. Does, read books, she does
     4. Does, go jogging, he doesn't
     5. Does, walk his dog, he does
     6. Does, ride his bike, he does

LEVEL UP   p.60

A 1. He doesn't wear
     2. Do they raise, Yes, they do
     3. I don't read
     4. Do we need, No, we don't
     5. doesn't taste bitter
     6. Does, freeze, No, it doesn't

B 1. Do, fight
     2. They don't like
     3. Do, feel happy
     4. don't speak Japanese
     5. Does he work
     6. doesn't like cloudy days
     7. don't bark
     8. Do you ride
     9. He doesn't miss
    10. Does, hurt
    11. don't sing, often
    12. monster doesn't have

1. doesn't play   **2.** wear   **3.** Yes, she does.
4. ②   **5.** ③   **6.** ②   **7.** ④   **8.** ①   **9.** ③   **10.** ②
11. ③   **12.** ④   **13.** Grace does not[doesn't] work on weekends.   **14.** Does this train go to Gwangju?   **15.** he doesn't, Yes, she does, Yes, they do

1 주어가 3인칭 단수이므로 일반동사의 부정문에 doesn't를 쓴다.

2 안경을 쓰고 있으므로 일반동사의 긍정문이 알맞다.

3 의문문에 대한 긍정 대답은 「Yes, 주어 + do[does].」로 나타낸다.

4 ② 일반동사(eat)의 부정문이고, doesn't가 쓰였으므로 주어는 3인칭 단수여야 한다.

5 ③ 일반동사(like)의 의문문이고, 주어가 2인칭 복수이므로 빈칸에는 Do가 와야 한다.

6 ② Does로 시작하는 일반동사의 의문문은 does를 사용해서 답한다.

7 ④ 주어가 2인칭인 일반동사의 의문문에 대한 대답에는 do를 써서 대답한다. 문맥상 부정의 대답이 와야 한다.

8 ② Does → Do ③ Do → Does ④ sells → sell

9 ① wants → want ② don't → doesn't ④ Does → Do

10 ② 첫 번째 문장은 주어(I)가 1인칭이므로 일반동사의 부정문에는 don't를 쓴다. 두 번째 문장은 일반동사(do)의 의문문이고, 주어(Alex)가 3인칭 단수이므로 빈칸에는 Does가 와야 한다.

11 ①②④ Does[does], ③ do

12 ④ 영어를 가르치냐는 질문에 긍정으로 대답하고 수학을 가르친다는 내용이 이어지는 것은 어색하다.

13 「3인칭 단수 주어 + does not[doesn't] + 동사원형 ~.」

14 「Does + 3인칭 단수 주어 + 동사원형 ~?」

15 주어가 3인칭 단수인 일반동사의 의문문에는 Does를 쓰며, 대답할 때도 does를 쓴다. 주어가 3인칭 복수인 일반동사의 의문문에 대답할 때는 do를 쓴다.

1. ④   **2.** ①   **3.** ④   **4.** ③   **5.** ②   **6.** ②   **7.** ③
8. ②   **9.** ④   **10.** ③   **11.** ②   **12.** ③   **13.** ①
14. ③   **15.** ②   **16.** ④   **17.** ②   **18.** ①   **19.** ③
20. I do not[don't] have long hair now.
21. The dog does not[doesn't] bite people.
22. Does Paul live in this neighborhood?, he does   **23.** (1) sells (2) doesn't open (3) closes

1 ④ -ch로 끝나는 동사의 3인칭 단수형은 -es를 붙여서 만든다. (catchs → catches)

2 ① have의 3인칭 단수형은 불규칙으로 변하는 형태로 has이다.

3 ④ on weekends로 반복되는 습관을 나타내므로 빈칸에는 일반동사인 play가 들어가야 하는데, 주어가 3인칭 단수이므로 plays가 알맞다.

4 ③ 일반동사(like)의 부정문이고, doesn't가 쓰였으므로 주어는 3인칭 단수여야 한다.

5 ② 주어가 복수일 경우 일반동사의 부정문은 「주어 + don't + 동사원형 ~.」으로 쓴다.

6 ② 일반동사(go)의 의문문이고, Does가 쓰였으므로 주어는 3인칭 단수만 들어갈 수 있다.

7 ③ 주어가 3인칭 단수이므로 동사원형인 like는 올 수 없다.

8 ② 주어가 복수일 때 일반동사의 부정문과 의문문에는 do를 쓴다.

9 ④ washs → washes

10 ③ don't → doesn't

11 ② Does로 시작하는 일반동사의 의문문은 does를 사용해서 답한다.

12 ①②④ does[Does], ③ Do

13 ②③④ Do[do], ① does

14 ③ 주어(She)가 3인칭 단수이므로 takes를 쓴다. 주어(Rabbits)가 복수이므로 동사원형을 쓴다.

15 ② 주어가 3인칭 단수일 때 의문문은 「Does + 주어 + 동사원형 ~?」의 형태로 쓰며, 의문문에 답할 때도 does를 이용한다.

16 ④ 주어가 3인칭 단수일 때는 일반동사도 3인칭 단수형으로, 주어가 복수일 때는 동사원형으로 쓴다.

17 ② cooks → cook

18 ① don't → doesn't

19 ③ Does → Do

20 「주어 + do not[don't] + 동사원형 ~.」

21 「3인칭 단수 주어 + does not[doesn't] + 동사원형 ~.」

22 「Does + 3인칭 단수 주어 + 동사원형 ~?」
「Yes, 주어 + does.」

23 주어가 3인칭 단수이므로 일반동사의 3인칭 단수형을 쓰고, 부정문은 doesn't를 이용한다.

Chapter 03   be동사의 과거형

Unit 01   be동사의 과거형 (1)

CHECK UP   p.73

A   **1.** V   **2.** X   **3.** V   **4.** V   **5.** X   **6.** V   **7.** X

B   **1.** was   **2.** were   **3.** was   **4.** were   **5.** was   **6.** was   **7.** were

<table><tr><td>Unit 02</td><td>be동사의 과거형 (2)</td></tr></table>

CHECK UP
p.75

A 1. ⓑ 2. ⓑ 3. ⓐ 4. ⓐ

B 1. is 2. was 3. were 4. are 5. was
6. was

LET'S PRACTICE 1
p.76

A 1. ⓑ 2. ⓐ 3. ⓐ 4. ⓑ 5. ⓐ 6. ⓑ

B 1. was 2. were 3. was 4. were
5. were

LET'S PRACTICE 2
p.77

A 1. were, ⓐ 2. was, ⓑ 3. were, ⓑ
4. is, ⓐ 5. was, ⓑ 6. is, ⓐ 7. were, ⓑ

해석 1 그 쿠키들은 달콤했다.
2 그 남자는 하키 선수였다.
3 그들은 놀이공원에 있었다.
4 그것은 Dave의 재킷이다.
5 그는 어제 경찰서에 있었다.
6 Richard는 모두에게 친절하다.
7 그녀의 양말은 상자 안에 있었다.

B 1. was 2. is 3. were 4. were
5. was 6. are 7. was

STEP UP 1
p.78

A 1. were 2. was 3. was 4. were
5. was 6. were 7. was 8. were
9. was 10. were 11. was 12. were

B 1. is, was 2. are, were 3. is, was
4. are, were 5. am, was 6. are, were
7. are, were 8. is, was 9. is, was

STEP UP 2
p.80

A 1. was 2. were 3. was 4. was
5. were 6. was 7. were 8. was
9. were 10. were

B 1. were cold 2. was big 3. were clean
4. cat was 5. was surprised
6. plants were

STEP UP 3
p.82

A 1. was on the desk
2. was very busy yesterday
3. were in the department store
4. were my grandmother's
5. were confident at that time
6. were hungry last night
7. was in the zoo
8. was kind to everyone
9. was in China before
10. were very nervous

B 1. I was at the mall the day before yesterday.
2. They are at the police station now.
3. The band was at the festival a month ago.
4. Sarah and Anna were neighbors last year.
5. My brother is in a restaurant now.
6. She was a guitarist at that time.
7. The doctors were in Africa in 2010.
8. My cat was on the bed last night.
9. The boys were best friends before.
10. I am at the amusement park right now.

STEP UP 4
p.84

A 1. It was snowy last night.
2. The water was very cold an hour ago.
3. My puppies were sick last month.
4. They were kids at that time.
5. His room was clean yesterday morning.
6. They were elementary school students in 2020.
7. The girl was a soccer player a few years ago.
8. My nephew was 11 years old last year.
9. The men were famous artists before.
10. Your shoes were under the bed a few minutes ago.

B 1. was dirty 2. is clean
3. were on the floor 4. are on the shelf

C 1. The tray was on the table.
2. The new game was fun.
3. Her stories were scary.
4. Those were my favorite dolls.

LEVEL UP
p.86

A 1. was on the table 2. Yesterday was
3. elephants were, zoo 4. was, a few
5. leaves were green 6. They are, now

B 1. was, last night
2. was cloudy, Sunday
3. We were nervous
4. were sick last week
5. room was clean
6. was a writer
7. cookies were sweet
8. was, at that time
9. necklace was my
10. are, park now
11. Her stories were
12. I am, amusement park

Unit 03 be동사 과거형의 부정문

CHECK UP
p.89

A 1. V 2. X 3. V 4. X 5. X 6. V 7. V

B 1. ⓑ 2. ⓑ 3. ⓒ 4. ⓑ 5. ⓑ 6. ⓑ 7. ⓑ

Unit 04 be동사 과거형의 의문문

CHECK UP
p.91

A 1. ⓐ 2. ⓑ 3. ⓑ 4. ⓐ 5. ⓑ

B 1. wasn't 2. No 3. Were, were
4. Were, Yes

LET'S PRACTICE 1
p.92

A 1. was not, wasn't 2. were not, weren't
3. was not, wasn't 4. were not, weren't
5. was not, wasn't

B 1. weren't[were not] 2. wasn't[was not]
3. wasn't[was not] 4. weren't[were not]
5. wasn't[was not] 6. weren't[were not]

LET'S PRACTICE 2
p.93

A 1. Was 2. Were 3. Were 4. Was
5. Was 6. Were

B 1. were 2. wasn't[was not]
3. wasn't[was not] 4. were
5. weren't[were not] 6. was

STEP UP 1
p.94

A 1. was, wasn't 2. were, weren't
3. was, wasn't 4. were, weren't
5. was, wasn't 6. was, wasn't
7. were, weren't 8. were, weren't
9. was, wasn't

B 1. Was she 2. Were the actors
3. Were you 4. Was my sister
5. Was James 6. Were the puppies
7. Was the living room 8. Were the students

STEP UP 2
p.96

A 1. Were[were] 2. wasn't
3. weren't 4. Was
5. wasn't 6. weren't
7. Was[was] 8. Were[were]
9. were 10. Was

B 1. they weren't 2. was not
3. Yes, were 4. weren't
5. wasn't 6. Were, was

STEP UP 3
p.98

A 1. weren't[were not] 2. weren't[were not]
3. O 4. Were
5. O 6. wasn't[was not]
7. was 8. O
9. wasn't[was not] 10. was

B 1. Sarah and Jim weren't in the same class.
2. Was she at the meeting yesterday?
3. The musical wasn't funny.
4. Were they in Korea in 2018?
5. The directors weren't famous before.
6. Were the students on the train?
7. The comic book wasn't on your desk.
8. We weren't tired yesterday.
9. Was Dan at home last night?
10. The turtles weren't on the beach.

A
1. My coach wasn't busy yesterday.
2. Were you in the hospital last week?
3. They weren't in Busan last month.
4. The skirt wasn't my sister's.
5. Was Tom a baseball player two years ago?
6. My brother wasn't in Europe last year.
7. Was the movie interesting?
8. Were your parents in Paris in 2019?
9. The weather wasn't windy yesterday.
10. Were those artists actors before?

B
1. The apples were not[weren't] fresh
2. Was he kind
3. I was not[wasn't] alone
4. was not[wasn't] cheap
5. Were their stories

C
1. was not smart
2. Were the kids absent
3. Were you tired
4. was not bored
5. Was she on the subway

LEVEL UP   p.102

A
1. was not boring
2. Was, bread, was
3. My brother wasn't tall
4. Were, soccer players, they weren't
5. kids weren't, last week
6. Was, new book

B
1. Were they, at that time
2. tomato wasn't fresh
3. Was, warm yesterday
4. We weren't busy
5. Was, bed, it was
6. were not colorful
7. wasn't, comedian
8. Were, kids[children], they were
9. students weren't absent
10. wasn't here before
11. Were, this morning
12. Was, heavy

Chapter 03 REVIEW TEST   p.104

1. are, were   **2.** is, was   **3.** Are, Were   **4.** ②
5. ③   **6.** ③   **7.** ④   **8.** ①   **9.** ③   **10.** ②
11. ④   **12.** ②   **13.** I was not[wasn't] sleepy at that time.   **14.** Were → Was   **15.** was, wasn't, is, is

1 주어가 We이므로 현재시제일 때는 are, 과거시제일 때는 were를 쓴다.
2 주어가 3인칭 단수이므로 현재시제일 때는 is, 과거시제일 때는 was를 쓴다.
3 주어가 you이므로 현재시제일 때는 Are, 과거시제일 때는 Were를 쓴다.
4 ② be동사 과거형의 부정문: 주어 + was[were] + not ~
5 ③ 첫 번째 문장은 be동사 현재시제의 의문문, 두 번째 문장은 be동사 과거시제의 부정문이다.
6 ③ 주어가 3인칭 단수이고 과거를 나타내는 부정문이므로 wasn't를 쓴다.
7 ①②③ were[Were], ④ was
8 ① 주어(the test)가 단수이므로 대명사 it과 was를 써서 답한다.
9 ③ right now(지금 당장)는 현재시제에서 쓰는 표현이다.
10 ① weren't → wasn't ③ wasn't → weren't ④ Was → Were
11 ④ 주어(The song)가 단수이므로 were를 was로 고쳐야 한다.
12 ①③④ '(~에) 있었다', ② '~이었다'
13 be동사 과거형의 부정문: 주어 + was[were] + not ~
14 과거를 나타내는 문장이고 주어(the music)가 단수이므로 Were를 Was로 고쳐야 한다.
15 two years ago, at that time은 과거형과 함께 쓰는 표현이고, now는 현재형과 함께 쓰는 표현이며, 주어(Andy, he)가 단수이므로 각각 was, wasn't, is, is를 쓴다.

Chapter 04   There + be동사

Unit 01   「There + be동사」의 현재형과 과거형

CHECK UP   p.111

A   1. ⓑ   2. ⓐ   3. ⓑ   4. ⓐ   5. ⓑ   6. ⓐ

B   1. is   2. are   3. were   4. was   5. is
6. are   7. was

CHECK UP　p.113

A　1. ⓑ　2. ⓑ　3. ⓑ　4. ⓐ　5. ⓐ　6. ⓑ　7. ⓑ

B　1. ⓑ　2. ⓑ　3. ⓑ　4. ⓐ　5. ⓑ　6. ⓐ

LET'S PRACTICE 1　p.114

A　1. juice, bread, a rainbow, a bird, a fish
　　2. children, trees, oranges, flowers, mirrors

B
1. There was
2. There were
3. There was
4. There was
5. There were
6. There was
7. There were
8. There were

LET'S PRACTICE 2　p.115

A
1. There weren't
2. There wasn't
3. There isn't
4. There isn't
5. There weren't
6. There aren't

B　1. O　2. X　3. X　4. O　5. X

STEP UP 1　p.116

A
1. There is
2. There wasn't
3. Is there
4. There were
5. There are
6. There weren't
7. Are there
8. There isn't
9. There aren't
10. Were there

B
1. There were
2. Were there
3. There aren't
4. Is there
5. There are
6. There was
7. There weren't
8. Are there
9. There isn't
10. There is

STEP UP 2　p.118

A
1. there wasn't
2. Yes, there
3. there isn't
4. Are there
5. there weren't
6. there aren't
7. Was there
8. there weren't
9. there are
10. there was

B
1. There are oranges
2. isn't a puppy
3. There aren't, grapes

---

4. Are there leaves
5. There were houses
6. There is pasta

STEP UP 3　p.120

A
1. There aren't, shoes
2. There is a cat
3. There wasn't a plant
4. Are there many insects
5. There were chickens
6. There isn't, money
7. There are clouds
8. Were there candles
9. There wasn't a notebook
10. Was there a ladder

B
1. There are two rainbows
2. There was a hamster
3. There weren't any customers
4. There aren't any fish
5. There were two dishes
6. There is a carpet
7. There wasn't any water
8. Is there tea
9. Are there old buildings
10. Were there many clothes

STEP UP 4　p.122

A
1. Is there a movie poster on the wall?
2. There aren't many books on the desk.
3. There was yogurt in the bowl.
4. There isn't a closet in the room.
5. There were tomatoes in the refrigerator.
6. There weren't many sheep on the hill.
7. Was there a wallet in this bag?
8. Are there children at the amusement park?
9. There wasn't a trash can on the beach.
10. Were there elephants in the zoo?

B
1. There is a French restaurant downtown.
2. Is there a baseball stadium in this city?
3. Were there many bikes on the street?
4. There were many tourists on the island.
5. Was there a basketball team in this school?
6. There was a smartphone under the sofa.
7. There weren't any monkeys in the zoo.
8. There are toys in my room.

9. There wasn't a department store in my town.
10. There aren't any toothbrushes in the bathroom.

LEVEL UP
p.124

A
1. There were toys
2. There aren't, children[kids]
3. there were
4. There wasn't, trash can
5. Is there, baseball stadium
6. There was a smartphone

B
1. Are there turtles
2. There was a doll
3. There weren't, monkeys
4. There are chairs
5. Were there many holidays
6. There isn't, rainbow
7. There wasn't, juice
8. Is there oil
9. There were cows
10. There is, bird
11. There aren't, shoes
12. Was there, school

Chapter 04 REVIEW TEST
p.126

1. is 2. are 3. was 4. ④ 5. ③ 6. ③
7. ④ 8. ③ 9. ③ 10. ② 11. ① 12. ②
13. There were many birds in the tree.
14. Were there tigers in the zoo? 15. No, there aren't., No, there isn't., Yes, there are.

1 coffee는 셀 수 없는 명사이므로 is를 쓴다.
2 flowers는 복수이므로 are를 쓴다.
3 a polar bear는 단수이므로 was를 쓴다.
4 ④ 빈칸 뒤의 명사 bananas는 복수이므로 There were가 알맞다.
5 ③ Is there ~?의 의문문에는 Yes, there is. 또는 No, there isn't.로 답한다.
6 ③ 빈칸 뒤의 a bakery는 단수, water는 셀 수 없는 명사이고 첫 번째 문장에 과거를 나타내는 표현(before)이 있으므로 was[Was]가 알맞다.
7 ①②③ is[Is], ④ are
8 ③ wasn't → weren't
9 ③ There is 뒤에는 복수명사가 올 수 없다.
10 ② 첫 번째 문장의 a piece of cake는 단수이므로 is가 적절하고, 두 번째 문장의 many tourists는 복수이고 뒤에 과거를 나타내는 표현이 있으므로 Were가 적절하다.
11 ① 과거를 나타내는 표현이 있으므로 is를 was로 고쳐야 한다.

12 ② money는 셀 수 없는 명사이고, 과거시제의 부정문이 되어야 하므로 There wasn't ~를 이용해 쓴다.
13 「There were + 복수명사」의 어순으로 쓴다.
14 「There + be동사」의 의문문은 「be동사 + there ~?」의 어순으로 쓴다.
15 Are there ~?의 의문문에는 Yes, there are. 또는 No, there aren't.로 답하고, Is there ~?의 의문문에는 Yes, there is. 또는 No, there isn't.로 답한다.

실전 Test 02회
p.130

1. ① 2. ② 3. ③ 4. ② 5. ④ 6. ④ 7. ④
8. ③ 9. ④ 10. ③ 11. ② 12. ③ 13. ③
14. ② 15. ④ 16. ① 17. ④ 18. ②
19. (1) Was the game really exciting at that time?
(2) There is not[isn't] a lamp on the desk.
20. Were there many people at the mall?
21. was → were 22. (1) There was (2) There wasn't (3) There is (4) There aren't

1 ① cheese는 셀 수 없는 명사이므로 is가 알맞다.
2 ② 주어가 3인칭 단수이고 과거를 나타내는 표현이 있으므로 was가 적절하다.
3 ③ 주어가 you인 과거시제 문장이므로 대답에는 were가 들어가야 한다.
4 ② a clock은 단수이고, 동사가 과거형이 되어야 하므로 There was를 이용해 쓴다.
5 ④ There aren't 다음에는 단수명사가 올 수 없다.
6 ④ 주어가 단수이므로 복수형 동사는 올 수 없다.
7 ④ many apples와 주어 They가 모두 복수이고 과거를 나타내는 표현이 있으므로 Were[were]가 적절하다.
8 ③ some clothes는 복수이므로 are가 되어야 한다.
9 ④ 주어(The tomato soup)가 셀 수 없는 명사이므로 weren't를 wasn't로 고쳐야 한다.
10 ①②④ Are[are], ③ Is
11 ①③④ was[Was], ② were
12 ①②④ '~이었다', ③ '(~에) 있었다'
13 ③ penguins는 복수이므로 Are를 쓰고, a mirror는 단수이므로 isn't를 쓴다.
14 ② 주어가 단수인 과거시제 문장이므로 be동사 was를 이용한다.
15 ④ a café가 단수이고 뒤에 과거를 나타내는 표현이 있으므로 wasn't, some olive oil이 셀 수 없는 명사이므로 Is로 고쳐야 한다.
16 ① was → were
17 ④ not were → were not[weren't]
18 ② 주어(the cookies)가 복수이므로 Yes, they were.라고 답해야 한다.
19 (1) be동사 과거형의 의문문: Was[Were] + 주어 ~?
(2) There is의 부정문은 is 뒤에 not을 붙여 만든다.
20 「There + be동사」의 의문문은 「be동사 + there ~?」의 어순으로 쓴다.

21 주어가 복수인 과거시제 문장이므로 was를 were로 고쳐야 한
다.

22 (1)~(2) 뒤에 단수명사가 이어지며 과거시제이므로 There was
와 There wasn't를 쓴다.

(3) 뒤에 단수명사가 이어지며 현재시제이므로 There is를 쓴
다.

(4) 뒤에 복수명사가 이어지며 현재시제이므로 There aren't
를 쓴다.

총괄평가 01회

1. ⑤　**2.** ②　**3.** ⑤　**4.** ③　**5.** ③　**6.** ③　**7.** ④
8. ②　**9.** ②　**10.** ⑤　**11.** ①　**12.** ③　**13.** ②
14. ④　**15.** ③　**16.** weren't, were　**17.** drys →
dries　**18.** has → does　**19.** Were there many
trees on the street?　**20.** She does not like sad
music.

총괄평가 02회

1. ③　**2.** ④　**3.** ②　**4.** ②　**5.** ⑤　**6.** ③　**7.** ②
8. ②　**9.** ④　**10.** ④　**11.** ③　**12.** ①　**13.** ④
14. ③　**15.** ①　**16.** My cat doesn't have a long
tail.　**17.** Were there many goats on the farm?
18. She knows my name.　**19.** There is
20. don't → doesn't

초등

Grammar
Inside

**Workbook
Answer Key**

2

Unit 01 - 02

WORD PRACTICE 2   p.4

A 1. shout 2. forget 3. screen
4. medicine 5. shark 6. ocean

B 1. soft 2. college 3. answer 4. shine
5. loudly

C

1. bamboo 2. candle 3. cloud
4. rope 5. pull 6. quietly

GRAMMAR PRACTICE 1   p.6

A 1. play 2. looks 3. hate 4. helps
5. love 6. have 7. wash 8. wear
9. need 10. use

B 1. ⓐ 2. ⓑ 3. ⓐ 4. ⓐ 5. ⓐ 6. ⓑ 7. ⓑ

GRAMMAR PRACTICE 2   p.8

A 1. feel 2. eat 3. needs 4. sleep
5. bake 6. looks 7. likes 8. drive
9. hates 10. learn 11. reads 12. love

B 1. taste 2. walk 3. fly 4. answers
5. meets 6. get up 7. dance 8. grows
9. play 10. hates 11. work 12. wear

GRAMMAR PRACTICE 3   p.10

A 1. do 2. plays 3. ride 4. want
5. sounds 6. moves 7. sings 8. save
9. looks 10. stay

B 1. Anna and Jack run fast.
2. I take a guitar class on Fridays.
3. She learns English these days.
4. You use too much water.
5. Sharks live in the ocean.
6. Carl buys his clothes at the mall.
7. The cake smells so delicious.
8. He visits his uncle every summer.
9. The speakers work well.
10. Jason eats pizza on Saturdays.

GRAMMAR PRACTICE 4   p.12

A 1. Dora speaks
2. This hamburger tastes
3. Snow comes
4. I borrow
5. Bella and Larry work
6. Kate writes
7. drinks tea
8. Those candles smell
9. He takes
10. They go
11. Josh loves
12. I bake cookies for her.
13. She borrows books from the library.
14. I drink coffee after lunch.
15. Amy works at the hospital.
16. I take photos[pictures] every day.
17. I go to school by subway.

Unit 03 - 04

WORD PRACTICE 2   p.16

A 1. train 2. chopsticks 3. swan
4. airport 5. pass 6. gym

B 1. scratch 2. relax 3. stomachache
4. worm 5. hometown

C

y	s	h	o	u	l	d	e	r	c
i	r	c	f	x	t	c	s	s	l
n	t	b	p	b	u	n	e	h	a
w	a	t	e	r	m	e	l	o	n
e	i	o	n	i	t	k	g	u	s
r	l	s	g	d	l	f	e	e	d
b	g	l	u	g	e	i	l	d	a
o	b	r	i	e	g	x	l	e	t

1. watermelon   **2.** tail   **3.** feed
4. shoulder   **5.** bridge   **6.** fix

GRAMMAR PRACTICE 1 p.18

A   1. ⓐ   2. ⓑ   3. ⓑ   4. ⓑ   5. ⓐ   6. ⓐ
7. ⓑ   8. ⓑ   9. ⓐ   10. ⓑ

B   1. ⓐ   2. ⓑ   3. ⓑ   4. ⓐ   5. ⓐ   6. ⓐ   7. ⓐ

GRAMMAR PRACTICE 2 p.20

A   1. sleep   2. drinks   3. shine   4. eat
5. have   6. goes   7. do   8. catches
9. saves   10. jumps   11. drives   12. studies

B   1. rains   2. tastes   3. take   4. teaches
5. scratches   6. reads   7. look   8. plays
9. flies   10. walk   11. has   12. does

GRAMMAR PRACTICE 3 p.22

A   1. miss   2. study   3. sits   4. wash
5. makes   6. remembers   7. touch
8. does   9. lives   10. fixes

B   1. She crosses the road.
2. The glue dries so fast.
3. Terry grows some tomatoes.
4. His pictures catch my eye.
5. They feel lonely.
6. He mixes salt and flour.
7. Gina often forgets their names.
8. My mom likes my photos.
9. The man carries heavy boxes every day.
10. We live in a big city.

GRAMMAR PRACTICE 4 p.24

A   1. She goes   2. Penguins walk
3. Meg washes   4. Ann pays
5. He eats   6. The candy tastes
7. I want   8. Mia has
9. A dog follows   10. My daughter uses
11. Engineers fix
12. I pay ten[10] dollars every week.
13. They eat some bread for breakfast.
14. Alex wants a blue shirt.
15. He fixes old bikes.
16. We go to the restaurant every day.
17. I wash my feet with soap.

Chapter 02 일반동사의 부정문과 의문문

Unit 01 - 02

WORD PRACTICE 2 p.28

A   1. bark   2. skate   3. fight   4. letter
5. football   6. dentist

B   1. trust   2. bookstore   3. answer
4. classical music   5. address

C

c	p	f	l	l	d	w	e	r	q
a	b	r	m	b	o	o	s	o	u
b	j	o	g	g	i	n	g	w	i
b	h	g	r	c	l	i	m	b	y
a	g	a	p	a	e	w	k	h	y
g	i	z	b	w	i	t	c	h	l
e	g	l	d	b	e	d	l	e	y
b	l	g	i	r	a	f	f	e	t

1. jogging   **2.** frog   **3.** climb
4. witch   **5.** cabbage   **6.** giraffe

GRAMMAR PRACTICE 1 p.30

A   1. doesn't   2. Do   3. work   4. Does
5. doesn't   6. sell   7. Do   8. don't
9. doesn't   10. Does, does   11. Do, don't

B
1. Do they go, they do
2. Does he like, he doesn't
3. Do you know, don't
4. Does, hurt, it does
5. Does she play, she does
6. Do you cook, don't
7. Do, climb, they do

GRAMMAR PRACTICE 2 p.32

A
1. don't like
2. doesn't have
3. don't jump
4. doesn't start
5. doesn't taste
6. doesn't exercise
7. doesn't tell
8. don't know
9. don't eat
10. doesn't look

B
1. Does she drink
2. Do they play
3. Does he want
4. Does Andy get
5. Do we need
6. Do people look
7. Does Kate help
8. Does the bookstore sell
9. Does Tiffany have
10. Do Emily and Dan fight

GRAMMAR PRACTICE 3 p.34

A
1. go, don't go
2. gets up, Does Nick get up
3. studies, doesn't study
4. have, don't have
5. eat, Do giraffes eat
6. starts, Does it start

B
1. Koalas don't eat fish.
2. My dogs don't bark at all.
3. Do they raise goats?
4. Does water freeze at 100℃?
5. The monster doesn't have a big mouth.
6. Do you watch TV at night?
7. We don't need a small bowl.
8. Do your parents have a car?
9. My friend doesn't like cloudy days.
10. Does the movie end at 5:00 p.m.?

GRAMMAR PRACTICE 4 p.36

A
1. Does she live
2. He doesn't read
3. They don't exercise
4. Does, feel
5. doesn't leave
6. Do, sleep

7. don't look
8. Do, know
9. Does, play
10. We don't like
11. doesn't trust
12. Does Eric exercise after work?
13. They don't[do not] live in Canada.
14. I don't[do not] read the newspaper every night.
15. This pillow doesn't[does not] feel soft.
16. Does she like chocolate cake?
17. We don't[do not] play basketball.

Chapter 03 be동사의 과거형

Unit 01 - 02

WORD PRACTICE 2 p.40

A
1. zoo
2. refrigerator
3. thirsty
4. sweet
5. confident
6. street

B
1. interesting
2. brave
3. surprised
4. salty
5. weather

C

s	p	f	l	l	d	w	e	r	q
n	e	r	v	o	u	s	s	o	y
n	j	e	s	y	u	c	e	w	v
a	h	s	r	k	r	i	u	e	e
r	g	h	p	s	h	e	l	f	s
m	i	e	b	p	l	n	u	p	l
y	g	l	d	h	e	t	r	a	y
s	c	i	e	n	t	i	s	t	t

1. nervous
2. army
3. fresh
4. scientist
5. shelf
6. tray

GRAMMAR PRACTICE 1 p.42

A
1. was
2. were
3. was
4. am
5. were
6. is
7. were
8. are
9. was
10. was
11. were
12. was

B
1. was
2. were
3. was
4. was
5. was
6. were
7. were
8. were
9. was
10. were
11. was
12. were

A
1. are, were
2. are, were
3. is, was
4. am, was
5. are, were
6. are, were
7. are, were
8. is, was
9. is, was
10. are, were

B
1. were neighbors last year
2. was a guitarist at that time
3. was on the bed last night
4. was at the mall the day before yesterday
5. were clean yesterday morning
6. were fun
7. were best friends before
8. was very cold an hour ago
9. was sick last month
10. were famous artists before

GRAMMAR PRACTICE 3   p.46

A
1. was surprised
2. was tasty
3. were small
4. was clean
5. is happy
6. was sunny
7. were nervous
8. are busy
9. were sweet
10. was boring

B
1. Those were my favorite dolls.
2. The street was very dirty.
3. We were students at that time.
4. The living room was dirty an hour ago.
5. I was a singer 10 years ago.
6. It was a boring book.
7. They were elementary school students in 2020.
8. The elephants were in the zoo.
9. My brother was hungry last night.
10. The waiters were very busy yesterday.

GRAMMAR PRACTICE 4   p.48

A
1. watch was
2. books were
3. were kind
4. was confident
5. was good
6. was, tired
7. were excited
8. was windy
9. was clean
10. was a doctor
11. leaves were
12. The pencil was on the desk.
13. The glasses were Peter's.
14. We were confident at that time.
15. He was kind to us.

16. They were doctors before.
17. Cathy was excited about the gifts.

Unit 03 - 04

WORD PRACTICE 2   p.52

A
1. meeting   2. delicious   3. train
4. comfortable   5. audience   6. animal

B
1. difficult   2. comic book   3. polite
4. director   5. cheap

C

s	b	e	a	c	h	w	e	w	c
h	r	c	f	x	t	c	s	a	l
e	h	o	s	p	i	t	a	l	a
a	a	t	e	r	r	e	l	l	n
v	i	o	n	e	o	k	g	e	s
y	m	s	g	p	o	c	u	t	h
c	o	l	o	r	f	u	l	b	e
n	o	i	e	o	g	e	l	e	m

1. beach   2. hospital   3. wallet
4. colorful   5. roof   6. heavy

GRAMMAR PRACTICE 1   p.54

A
1. were   2. Was   3. Were   4. wasn't
5. was not   6. weren't   7. Were   8. Was
9. Was   10. wasn't   11. were   12. weren't

B
1. Were   2. was   3. Were   4. were
5. Were   6. was   7. Was   8. Were
9. Were   10. was   11. was   12. Was

GRAMMAR PRACTICE 2   p.56

A
1. were, weren't
2. was, wasn't
3. were, weren't
4. was, wasn't
5. was, wasn't
6. were, weren't
7. was, wasn't
8. were, weren't
9. was, wasn't
10. was, wasn't

B
1. Was the weather
2. Were the bags
3. Was she
4. Were they
5. Was the test
6. Was Jim
7. Was the new sofa
8. Was the writer
9. Were the tables
10. Were the students

A
1. Were they good at English
2. The tomatoes were not fresh
3. Was the desk heavy
4. The flowers weren't colorful
5. Were those artists actors
6. Was it snowy
7. The books were not expensive
8. I was not a baseball player
9. Was his new book interesting
10. He was not a math teacher

B
1. The students weren't late for the class.
2. Were you at home last night?
3. The chair wasn't light.
4. They weren't polite to their teacher.
5. Was your room clean yesterday?
6. Was the food delicious there?
7. We weren't in Jeju-do yesterday.
8. Were their stories boring?
9. Were you at the museum?
10. It wasn't snowy in Busan last winter.

GRAMMAR PRACTICE 4   p.60

A
1. weren't famous   2. Was, interesting
3. wasn't snowy   4. turtles weren't
5. Were the kids
6. Were your parents, they weren't
7. Were you, was   8. book wasn't
9. Was Tom   10. wasn't busy
11. Were, healthy
12. Was Julia absent from school?
13. Was your cat healthy?
14. The singer wasn't[was not] famous before.
15. The comic books weren't[were not] on your desk.
16. They weren't[were not] busy last week.
17. The man wasn't[was not] on the beach.

Chapter 04   There + be동사

Unit 01 - 02

WORD PRACTICE 2   p.64

A
1. basket   2. closet   3. plant   4. ladder
5. drawer   6. toothbrush

B
1. island   2. fishbowl   3. cupboard
4. farm   5. theater

C

s	p	c	u	s	t	o	m	e	r
i	b	l	m	b	o	o	s	o	u
n	p	o	n	d	i	n	g	p	i
a	h	t	r	i	g	h	u	a	p
e	g	h	p	a	e	w	k	l	u
k	i	e	b	s	u	b	w	a	y
v	a	s	e	n	e	d	l	c	o
a	l	s	t	a	f	e	l	e	t

1. clothes   2. pond   3. customer
4. vase   5. subway   6. palace

GRAMMAR PRACTICE 1   p.66

A
1. is   2. Is   3. Were   4. were   5. Was
6. was   7. weren't   8. are   9. isn't
10. aren't   11. Were   12. was

B
1. are, Are there   2. was, Was there
3. is, Is there   4. was, Was there
5. were, Were there   6. is, Is there
7. are, Are there   8. were, Were there
9. are, Are there   10. was, Was there

GRAMMAR PRACTICE 2   p.68

A
1. There was a trash can
2. There are not many people
3. There were kids
4. Is there a good restaurant
5. There were two birds
6. There is not a department store
7. Was there a bank
8. There were many tourists

9. There were not any shoes
10. Is there a subway station

B 1. Are, there aren't 2. Is, there isn't
3. Were, there weren't 4. Are, there are
5. Were, there were 6. Was, there was
7. Were, there weren't 8. Was, there was
9. Is, there is 10. Are, there aren't

12. There weren't[were not] any fruits in the refrigerator.
13. There is a theater near here.
14. There were cookies on the plate.
15. There were many pens on the desk.
16. Is there a dish in the cupboard?
17. Was there dust on the roof?

GRAMMAR PRACTICE 3   p.70

A 1. There aren't many trees on this mountain.
2. Is there a laptop on the desk?
3. There were many singers at the festival.
4. Were there pigs on the farm?
5. There isn't a bank around here.
6. Were there many tourists at the palace?
7. There is butter in the refrigerator.
8. There was a mirror on the wall.
9. Was there a baseball team in this school?
10. There is a wallet in this bag.

B 1. There were cookies in a bowl.
2. There are not[aren't] any chairs in the room.
3. Were there many customers at the mall?
4. There is pasta on the plate.
5. Was there orange juice in the cup?
6. There aren't[are not] any flowers on the cake.
7. There were two singers on the stage.
8. There aren't[are not] any fish in the fishbowl.
9. There are toys on the floor.
10. Were there many holidays last year?

GRAMMAR PRACTICE 4   p.72

A 1. There is a school
2. Was there a ladder
3. There isn't a carpet
4. Are there cups
5. There weren't, muffins
6. There wasn't a plant
7. Were there, festivals
8. There was some bread
9. Is there oil
10. There wasn't, water
11. There were cows

MEMO

MEMO

MEMO

MEMO

MEMO

초등 Grammar Inside

Answer Key

대한민국 초등 어휘서의 기준

체계적인 쓰기 훈련으로 초등 어휘 완성

* 휴대용 미니북 별책 제공

1 새 교육과정에 따른 쓰기 활동 강화

단어 및 문장 쓰기 활동을 통한
암기력 향상과 쓰기 자신감 강화

2 반복 학습이 가능한 체계적인 설계

예문 내 어휘 누적 제시와 누적 테스트를 통한
반복 훈련으로 학습 완성도 향상

3 다양한 부가자료 및 디지털 서비스

빈틈없는 암기 학습을 위한 휴대용 미니북 및
효율적 학습을 위한 디지털 서비스 제공

BOOK LIST

도/서/목/록

초등영어 된다 시리즈

초등영어
리딩이 된다

교과 내용을 영어로 쉽고 재미있게
학습하는 초등 독해서
START 1 | 2 | 3 | 4
BASIC 1 | 2 | 3 | 4
JUMP 1 | 2 | 3 | 4

초등영어
문법이 된다

초등 교육과정을 기반으로 한 영문법 학습서
Starter 1 | Starter 2 | 1 | 2

초등영어
단어가 된다

교육부 권장 초등 필수 영단어 학습서
1 | 2 | 3 | 4

초등영어
파닉스가 된다

알파벳 음가 블렌딩 연습을 통해
읽기 유창성을 기르는 파닉스 학습서
1 | 2

초등영어
사이트 워드가 된다

영어 읽기 독립을 위한 사이트 워드 학습서
1 | 2

독해

Reading
TUTOR 리딩튜터

체계적인 초·중·고등 독해 프로그램
Starter 1 | 2 | 3
Junior 1 | 2 | 3 | 4
Challenger 1 | 2 | 3

달콤한 LITERACY (Reading)

초등학생을 위한 문해력 기본서
LEVEL 1 | 2 | 3
LEVEL 4 | 5 | 6

READING BUDDY

초등학생을 위한 독해 입문서
1 | 2 | 3
 Grammar Buddy | Listening Buddy

---

어휘

능률
VOCA

대한민국 어휘서의 표준
초등 기본 | 초등 필수
중등 기본 | 중등 필수
중등 고난도 | 중등 숙어
고등 기본 | 수능 필수 | 수능 고난도
어원편 중등 | 고등

해당 교재와 연계되는 시리즈

초등 Grammar Inside

Workbook

2

NE 능률

초등 Grammar Inside

Workbook

2

Ⓐ 다음 단어를 두 번씩 듣고 따라 쓴 후 그 뜻을 쓰세요.

단어	두 번 따라 쓰기		뜻 쓰기
quietly 조용하게			
forget 잊다			
soft 부드러운			
cloud 구름			
loudly 큰 소리로			
draw 그리다			
runny nose 콧물			
shine 빛나다			
screen 화면			
firefighter 소방관			
rope 밧줄			
arrive 도착하다			
work 일하다, 작동하다			

단어	두 번 따라 쓰기	뜻 쓰기
fever 열		
answer 대답하다		
stranger 낯선 사람		
save 구하다		
medicine 약		
candle 양초		
pull 당기다		
sled 썰매		
college 대학		
shark 상어		
ocean 바다		
shout 소리치다		
bamboo 대나무		

A 주어진 철자의 순서를 바르게 맞추어 우리말 뜻에 해당하는 단어를 쓰세요.

1 
tuhso
소리치다

2 
tofgre
잊다

3 
eerscn
화면

4 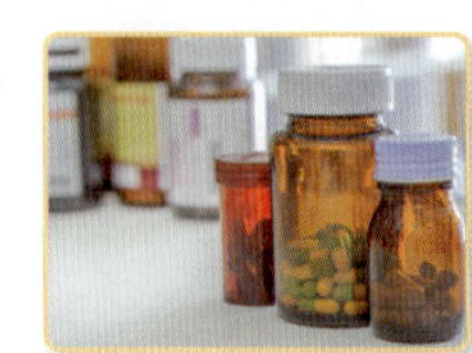
cemiedin
약

5 
arksh
상어

6 
eacon
바다

B 우리말과 같은 뜻이 되도록 보기 에서 알맞은 단어를 골라 쓰세요.

| 보기 | answer | shine | college | loudly | soft |

1 This towel feels ________________.   이 수건은 부드럽게 느껴진다.

2 My sister is a ________________ student.   나의 누나는 대학생이다.

3 Please ________________ my questions.   제 질문들에 답해 주세요.

4 The stars ________________ in the sky.   별들이 하늘에서 빛난다.

5 He plays the drums so ________________.   그는 매우 큰 소리로 드럼을 연주한다.

C 다음 사진에 해당하는 단어를 아래 퍼즐에서 찾아 ○ 표시하고 빈칸에 쓰세요.

s	p	c	l	l	d	w	e	r	q
i	b	a	m	b	o	o	s	o	u
n	j	n	s	y	u	w	e	w	i
a	h	d	r	k	r	a	u	e	e
e	g	l	p	e	r	o	p	e	t
r	i	e	b	p	l	n	u	p	l
b	g	l	d	h	e	d	l	e	y
c	l	o	u	d	s	w	l	a	t

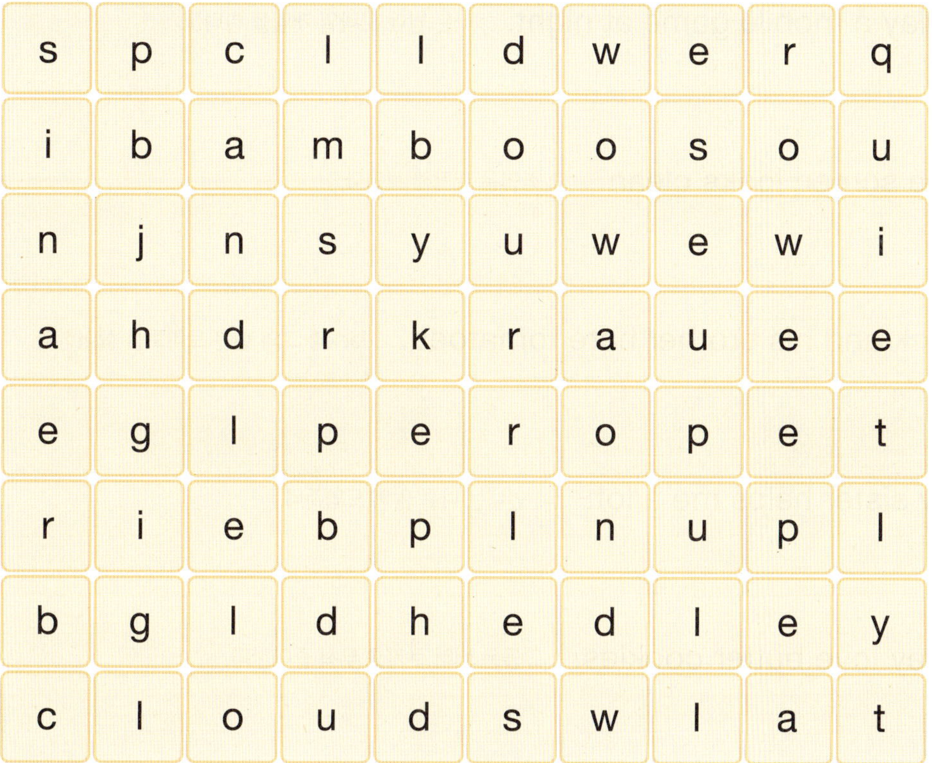

1 
대나무

2 
양초

3 
구름

4 
밧줄

5 
당기다

6 
조용하게

A 다음 문장에서 일반동사에 ○ 표시하세요.

1 I play a mobile game at night.   나는 밤에 모바일 게임을 한다.

2 The screen looks clean.   그 화면은 깨끗해 보인다.

3 Jack and his brother hate tomatoes.   Jack과 그의 형은 토마토를 싫어한다.

4 My sister helps me a lot.   내 언니는 나를 많이 도와준다.

5 They love butter cookies.   그들은 버터 쿠키를 무척 좋아한다.

6 Ants have six legs.   개미들은 여섯 개의 다리를 가지고 있다.

7 I wash my hands often.   나는 내 손을 자주 씻는다.

8 They wear uniforms on Mondays.   그들은 월요일마다 유니폼을 입는다.

9 I need a dictionary.   나는 사전이 필요하다.

10 Firefighters use masks and ropes.   소방관들은 마스크와 밧줄을 사용한다.

B 다음 중 맞는 문장을 고르세요.

1 ⓐ Cheetahs run very fast.　치타들은 매우 빠르게 달린다.

　　ⓑ Cheetahs runs very fast.

2 ⓐ I understands your idea.　나는 너의 생각을 이해한다.

　　ⓑ I understand your idea.

3 ⓐ He sleeps 10 hours a night.　그는 하룻밤에 10시간을 잔다.

　　ⓑ He sleep 10 hours a night.

4 ⓐ The moon shines brightly.　달은 밝게 빛난다.

　　ⓑ The moon shine brightly.

5 ⓐ Bears eat honey.　곰들은 꿀을 먹는다.

　　ⓑ Bears eats honey.

6 ⓐ Roy swim very well.　Roy는 수영을 매우 잘한다.

　　ⓑ Roy swims very well.

7 ⓐ She speak French.　그녀는 프랑스어를 한다.

　　ⓑ She speaks French.

A (   ) 안에서 알맞은 것을 고르세요.

1 I (feel / feels) really sorry for him.   나는 그가 매우 안쓰럽다고 느낀다.

2 Monkeys (eats / eat) bananas.   원숭이들은 바나나를 먹는다.

3 Cindy (need / needs) some pepper.   Cindy는 후추가 조금 필요하다.

4 Frogs (sleep / sleeps) during winter.   개구리들은 겨울 동안 잠을 잔다.

5 Bakers (bake / bakes) bread every morning.   제빵사들은 매일 아침 빵을 굽는다.

6 This mirror (look / looks) so dirty.   이 거울은 아주 더러워 보인다.

7 He (like / likes) action movies.   그는 액션 영화를 좋아한다.

8 They (drives / drive) very well.   그들은 운전을 매우 잘한다.

9 My cat (hate / hates) strangers.   내 고양이는 낯선 사람을 싫어한다.

10 Some students (learn / learns) history.   몇 명의 학생들은 역사를 배운다.

11 My father (read / reads) the newspaper every morning.
내 아버지는 매일 아침 신문을 읽으신다.

12 We (love / loves) our parents.   우리는 우리의 부모님을 사랑한다.

B 주어진 동사를 알맞은 현재형으로 바꿔 문장을 완성하세요.

1 Lemons ______________ sour. (taste)   레몬들은 신맛이 난다.

2 I ______________ my dog every day. (walk)   나는 매일 나의 개를 산책시킨다.

3 The birds ______________ to the west. (fly)   새들은 서쪽으로 날아간다.

4 Bora always ______________ quickly. (answer)   보라는 항상 빠르게 대답한다.

5 She ______________ Andy on Tuesdays. (meet)   그녀는 화요일마다 Andy를 만난다.

6 We ______________ early in the morning. (get up)   우리는 아침에 일찍 일어난다.

7 Those dancers ______________ beautifully. (dance)   저 댄서들은 아름답게 춤춘다.

8 This tree ______________ so fast. (grow)   이 나무는 아주 빠르게 자란다.

9 They ______________ hockey on Sundays. (play)   그들은 일요일마다 하키를 한다.

10 Hanna ______________ coffee. (hate)   Hanna는 커피를 싫어한다.

11 Tom and Meg ______________ at the library. (work)   Tom과 Meg는 도서관에서 일한다.

12 Kids ______________ heavy helmets. (wear)   아이들은 무거운 헬멧을 쓴다.

A 보기 에서 알맞은 단어를 골라 쓰세요. (필요하면 형태를 바꾸세요.)

보기	sound	do	stay	look	sing
	move	play	ride	want	save

1 Ian and Ted _______________ their homework every day.
Ian과 Ted는 매일 숙제를 한다.

2 Harry _______________ with robots.   Harry는 로봇들을 가지고 논다.

3 I _______________ a bike in the park.   나는 공원에서 자전거를 탄다.

4 We _______________ a bowl of salad.   우리는 샐러드 한 그릇을 원한다.

5 Your voice _______________ so soft.   너의 목소리는 아주 부드럽게 들린다.

6 The earth _______________ around the sun.   지구는 태양 주위에서 움직인다.

7 The woman _______________ a song every night.   그 여자는 매일 밤 노래를 부른다.

8 Firefighters _______________ many lives.   소방관들은 많은 생명을 구한다.

9 It _______________ like an interesting video.   그것은 흥미로운 영상처럼 보인다.

10 They _______________ home at night.   그들은 밤에 집에 있다.

B 밑줄 친 부분을 바르게 고쳐 문장을 다시 쓰세요.

1 Anna and Jack <u>runs</u> fast. Anna와 Jack은 빠르게 달린다.

➡ ____

2 I <u>takes</u> a guitar class on Fridays. 나는 금요일마다 기타 수업을 듣는다.

➡ ____

3 She <u>learn</u> English these days. 그녀는 요즘에 영어를 배운다.

➡ ____

4 You <u>uses</u> too much water. 너는 너무 많은 물을 쓴다.

➡ ____

5 Sharks <u>lives</u> in the ocean. 상어들은 바다에 산다.

➡ ____

6 Carl <u>buy</u> his clothes at the mall. Carl은 그의 옷을 쇼핑몰에서 산다.

➡ ____

7 The cake <u>smell</u> so delicious. 이 케이크는 아주 맛있는 냄새가 난다.

➡ ____

8 He <u>visit</u> his uncle every summer. 그는 매년 여름 그의 삼촌댁을 방문한다.

➡ ____

9 The speakers <u>works</u> well. 그 스피커들은 잘 작동한다.

➡ ____

10 Jason <u>eat</u> pizza on Saturdays. Jason은 토요일마다 피자를 먹는다.

➡ ____

A 우리말과 같은 뜻이 되도록 주어진 말을 이용하여 문장을 완성하세요.

1 Dora는 스페인어를 한다. (speak)

→ ______________ ______________ Spanish.

2 이 햄버거는 정말 맛있다. (this hamburger, taste)

→ ______________ ______________ ______________ really good.

3 눈은 구름으로부터 온다. (snow, come)

→ ______________ ______________ from clouds.

4 나는 도서관에서 책들을 빌린다. (borrow)

→ ______________ ______________ books from the library.

5 Bella와 Larry는 학교에서 일한다. (work)

→ ______________ ______________ ______________ ______________ at the

school.

6 Kate는 그를 위해 편지를 쓴다. (write)

→ ______________ ______________ a letter for him.

7 나의 아빠는 아침 식사 후에 차를 마신다. (drink, tea)

→ My dad ______________ ______________ after breakfast.

8 저 양초들은 냄새가 매우 좋다. (those candles, smell)

→ ______________ ______________ ______________ very good.

9 그는 매일 사진들을 찍는다. (take)

→ ______________ ______________ photos every day.

10 그들은 버스를 타고 학교에 간다. (go)

→ ______________ ______________ to school by bus.

11 Josh는 요가하는 것을 매우 좋아한다. (love)

→ ______________ ______________ doing yoga.

12 나는 그녀를 위해 쿠키를 굽는다. (bake cookies)

→ ____

13 그녀는 도서관에서 책들을 빌린다. (borrow)

→ ____

14 나는 점심 식사 후에 커피를 마신다. (coffee, lunch)

→ ____

15 Amy는 병원에서 일한다. (the hospital)

→ ____

16 나는 매일 사진들을 찍는다. (take)

→ ____

17 나는 지하철을 타고 학교에 간다. (subway)

→ ____

A 다음 단어를 두 번씩 듣고 따라 쓴 후 그 뜻을 쓰세요.

단어	두 번 따라 쓰기	뜻 쓰기
pass 건네주다		
fix 고치다		
touch 만지다, 닿다		
work 일, 일터		
shoulder 어깨		
tail 꼬리		
scratch 긁다		
train 훈련시키다		
feed 밥을 먹이다		
watermelon 수박		
relax 휴식을 취하다		
remember 기억하다		
grow 자라다, 키우다		

단어	두 번 따라 쓰기	뜻 쓰기
gym 체육관		
hometown 고향		
machine 기계		
bridge 다리		
cross 가로지르다, 건너다		
swan 백조		
finish 끝내다		
airport 공항		
worm 벌레		
piggy bank 돼지 저금통		
stomachache 복통		
chopsticks 젓가락		
noise 소음		

A 주어진 철자의 순서를 바르게 맞추어 우리말 뜻에 해당하는 단어를 쓰세요.

1 
atrni
훈련시키다

2
stisopchck
젓가락

3 
answ
백조

4 
trairop
공항

5
saps
건네주다

6
myg
체육관

B 우리말과 같은 뜻이 되도록 보기 에서 알맞은 단어를 골라 쓰세요.

> 보기   relax   hometown   stomachache   worm   scratch

1 Don't _______________ the leather.   가죽을 긁지 마라.

2 Just _______________ and enjoy your weekend.   그저 휴식을 취하고 주말을 즐겨라.

3 I have a terrible _______________.   나는 배가 몹시 아프다.

4 There is a _______________ in this apple.   이 사과 안에 벌레 한 마리가 있다.

5 He always misses his _______________.   그는 항상 그의 고향을 그리워한다.

C 다음 사진에 해당하는 단어를 아래 퍼즐에서 찾아 ○ 표시하고 빈칸에 쓰세요.

y	s	h	o	u	l	d	e	r	c
i	r	c	f	x	t	c	s	s	l
n	t	b	p	b	u	n	e	h	a
w	a	t	e	r	m	e	l	o	n
e	i	o	n	i	t	k	g	u	s
r	l	s	g	d	l	f	e	e	d
b	g	l	u	g	e	i	l	d	a
o	b	r	i	e	g	x	l	e	t

1

수박

2

꼬리

3

밥을 먹이다

4
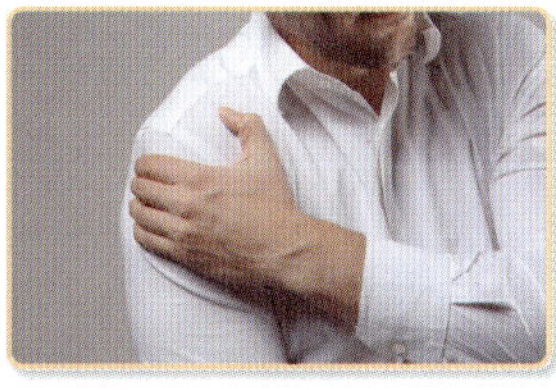
어깨

5

다리

6

고치다

A 다음 동사의 3인칭 단수형으로 알맞은 것을 고르세요.

1 say　　ⓐ says　　ⓑ saies

2 catch　　ⓐ catchs　　ⓑ catches

3 study　　ⓐ studys　　ⓑ studies

4 pass　　ⓐ passs　　ⓑ passes

5 mix　　ⓐ mixes　　ⓑ mixs

6 do　　ⓐ does　　ⓑ dos

7 buy　　ⓐ buies　　ⓑ buys

8 hurry　　ⓐ hurrys　　ⓑ hurries

9 have　　ⓐ has　　ⓑ haves

10 fix　　ⓐ fixs　　ⓑ fixes

B 다음 중 맞는 문장을 고르세요.

1 ⓐ The concert finishes at 11 o'clock. 그 콘서트는 11시에 끝난다.

　 ⓑ The concert finishs at 11 o'clock.

2 ⓐ I uses chopsticks very well. 나는 젓가락을 아주 잘 사용한다.

　 ⓑ I use chopsticks very well.

3 ⓐ My father actes on the stage. 내 아버지는 무대에서 연기하신다.

　 ⓑ My father acts on the stage.

4 ⓐ Jisu studies Spanish every morning. 지수는 매일 아침 스페인어를 공부한다.

　 ⓑ Jisu studyes Spanish every morning.

5 ⓐ Her smile shines brightly. 그녀의 미소는 밝게 빛난다.

　 ⓑ Her smile shine brightly.

6 ⓐ She drives to the airport. 그녀는 공항에 운전해서 간다.

　 ⓑ She drive to the airport.

7 ⓐ The bridge crosses the river. 그 다리는 강을 가로지른다.

　 ⓑ The bridge cross the river.

A ( ) 안에서 알맞은 것을 고르세요.

1 Bears (sleep / sleeps) in the winter. 곰들은 겨울에 잠을 잔다.

2 He (drink / drinks) a glass of juice in the morning. 그는 아침에 주스 한 잔을 마신다.

3 My new shoes (shines / shine) brightly. 나의 새 신발은 밝게 빛난다.

4 You (eat / eats) too much fast food. 너는 패스트푸드를 너무 많이 먹는다.

5 I (has / have) a tablet PC. 나는 태블릿 PC를 가지고 있다.

6 My sister (go / goes) to the bakery every day. 내 여동생은 매일 빵집에 간다.

7 Dan and Kate (do / does) their work at night. Dan과 Kate는 밤에 일을 한다.

8 The early bird (catchs / catches) the worm. 일찍 일어나는 새가 벌레를 잡는다.

9 It (save / saves) some time. 그것은 약간의 시간을 절약해 준다.

10 The puppy (jumpes / jumps) really high. 그 강아지는 아주 높게 점프한다.

11 Anna (drives / drive) to the mall. Anna는 쇼핑몰까지 운전해서 간다.

12 She (studys / studies) American history. 그녀는 미국 역사를 공부한다.

B 주어진 동사를 알맞은 현재형으로 바꿔 문장을 완성하세요.

1 It ________________ a lot in June. (rain) 6월에는 비가 많이 온다.

2 This candy ________________ like watermelon. (taste) 이 사탕은 수박 맛이 난다.

3 Lilly and Ben ________________ photos together. (take)
Lilly와 Ben은 함께 사진들을 찍는다.

4 My uncle ________________ math. (teach) 내 삼촌은 수학을 가르친다.

5 Her cat ________________ the wall. (scratch) 그녀의 고양이는 벽을 긁는다.

6 She ________________ the novel every day. (read) 그녀는 매일 그 소설을 읽는다.

7 You ________________ cold. (look) 너는 추워 보인다.

8 Stella ________________ baseball after school. (play) Stella는 방과 후에 야구를 한다.

9 The bird ________________ quickly. (fly) 그 새는 빠르게 난다.

10 We ________________ to school. (walk) 우리는 학교에 걸어간다.

11 Olivia ________________ four dresses. (have) Olivia는 드레스를 네 벌 가지고 있다.

12 He ________________ yoga in the evening. (do) 그는 저녁에 요가를 한다.

A 우리말과 같은 뜻이 되도록 보기 에서 알맞은 단어를 골라 쓰세요. (필요하면 형태를 바꾸세요.)

| 보기 | sit | do | make | fix | study |
| | remember | wash | live | miss | touch |

1 I _______________ the cafeteria in my hometown.
나는 내 고향에 있는 그 식당이 그립다.

2 We _______________ Chinese history.   우리는 중국 역사를 공부한다.

3 Joe _______________ next to me.   Joe는 내 옆에 앉는다.

4 They _______________ their feet in the bathroom.   그들은 욕실에서 발을 씻는다.

5 The machine _______________ a lot of noise.   그 기계는 많은 소음을 낸다.

6 Daniel _______________ his aunt.   Daniel은 그의 이모를 기억한다.

7 His hands _______________ the shelf.   그의 손은 선반에 닿는다.

8 She _______________ her homework at night.   그녀는 밤에 숙제를 한다.

9 Heidi _______________ in New York.   Heidi는 뉴욕에 산다.

10 He _______________ the roof.   그는 지붕을 고친다.

B 밑줄 친 부분을 바르게 고쳐 문장을 다시 쓰세요.

1 She <u>cross</u> the road.　그녀는 길을 건넌다.

➜ ____

2 The glue <u>drys</u> so fast.　그 접착제는 매우 빨리 마른다.

➜ ____

3 Terry <u>grow</u> some tomatoes.　Terry는 토마토를 조금 키운다.

➜ ____

4 His pictures <u>catchs</u> my eye.　그의 그림들은 내 눈길을 잡는다.

➜ ____

5 They <u>feels</u> lonely.　그들은 외롭다고 느낀다.

➜ ____

6 He <u>mixs</u> salt and flour.　그는 소금과 밀가루를 섞는다.

➜ ____

7 Gina often <u>forget</u> their names.　Gina는 자주 그들의 이름을 잊는다.

➜ ____

8 My mom <u>like</u> my photos.　우리 엄마는 내 사진들을 좋아한다.

➜ ____

9 The man <u>carrys</u> heavy boxes every day.　그 남자는 매일 무거운 상자들을 옮긴다.

➜ ____

10 We <u>lives</u> in a big city.　우리는 대도시에 산다.

➜ ____

A 우리말과 같은 뜻이 되도록 주어진 말을 이용하여 문장을 완성하세요.

1 그녀는 매일 체육관에 간다. (go)

→ _______________ _______________ to the gym every day.

2 펭귄들은 매우 빠르게 걷는다. (walk)

→ _______________ _______________ very fast.

3 Meg는 그녀의 손을 비누로 씻는다. (wash)

→ _______________ _______________ her hands with soap.

4 Ann은 매달 3달러를 지불한다. (pay)

→ _______________ _______________ three dollars every month.

5 그는 점심으로 빵을 조금 먹는다. (eat)

→ _______________ _______________ some bread for lunch.

6 그 사탕은 레몬 맛이 난다. (the candy, taste)

→ _______________ _______________ _______________ like lemon.

7 나는 노란색 운동화를 원한다. (want)

→ _______________ _______________ yellow sneakers.

8 Mia는 열이 있다. (have)

→ _______________ _______________ a fever.

9 개 한 마리가 너를 따라온다. (follow)

→ _____________ _____________ _____________ you.

10 내 딸은 숟가락과 포크를 사용한다. (daughter, use)

→ _____________ _____________ _____________ a spoon and a fork.

11 엔지니어들은 오래된 기계들을 고친다. (engineers, fix)

→ _____________ _____________ old machines.

12 나는 매주 10달러를 지불한다. (every week)

→ ____

13 그들은 아침으로 빵을 조금 먹는다. (eat, breakfast)

→ ____

14 Alex는 파란색 셔츠를 원한다. (a blue shirt)

→ ____

15 그는 오래된 자전거들을 고친다. (bikes)

→ ____

16 우리는 매일 그 식당에 간다. (the restaurant)

→ ____

17 나는 내 발을 비누로 씻는다. (my feet)

→ ____

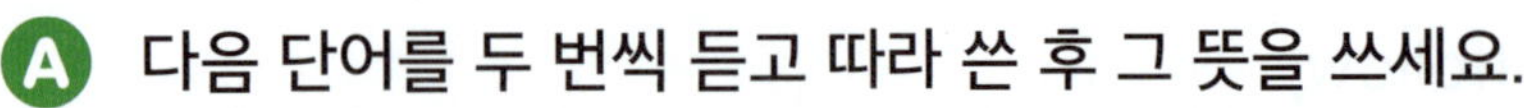

A 다음 단어를 두 번씩 듣고 따라 쓴 후 그 뜻을 쓰세요.

단어	두 번 따라 쓰기	뜻 쓰기
frog 개구리		
fit 꼭 맞다		
trust 신뢰하다		
truth 진실		
hurt 다치게 하다, 아프다		
football 풋볼		
climb 오르다		
miss 그리워하다		
bark 짖다		
bitter 맛이 쓴		
address 주소		
goat 염소		
giraffe 기린		

단어	두 번 따라 쓰기		뜻 쓰기
freeze 얼다			
classical music 클래식 음악			
fight 싸우다			
cabbage 양배추			
bookstore 서점			
witch 마녀			
letter 편지			
answer 정답			
horrible 무서운			
leave 떠나다			
skate 스케이트를 타다			
dentist 치과 의사			
jogging 조깅			

A 주어진 철자의 순서를 바르게 맞추어 우리말 뜻에 해당하는 단어를 쓰세요.

1 
abkr
짖다

2 
akste
스케이트를 타다

3 
gtfih
싸우다

4 
eeltrt
편지

5 
otblafol
풋볼

6 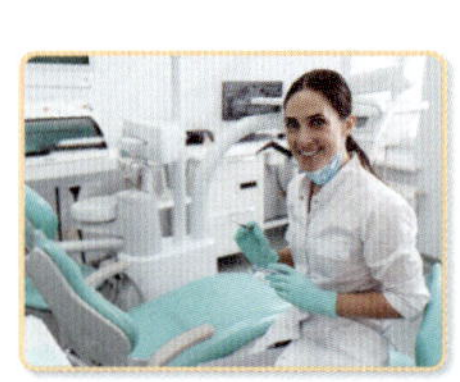
tneistd
치과 의사

B 우리말과 같은 뜻이 되도록 보기 에서 알맞은 단어를 골라 쓰세요.

보기   answer   address   trust   bookstore   classical music

1 I can't ______________ him anymore.   나는 더 이상 그를 신뢰할 수 없다.

2 The ______________ sells children's books.   그 서점은 어린이 도서를 판다.

3 This is not the right ______________.   이것은 올바른 정답이 아니다.

4 I listen to ______________ in the morning.   나는 아침에 클래식 음악을 듣는다.

5 What's your email ______________?   너의 이메일 주소가 뭐니?

C 다음 사진에 해당하는 단어를 아래 퍼즐에서 찾아 ○ 표시하고 빈칸에 쓰세요.

c	p	f	l	l	d	w	e	r	q
a	b	r	m	b	o	o	s	o	u
b	j	o	g	g	i	n	g	w	i
b	h	g	r	c	l	i	m	b	y
a	g	a	p	a	e	w	k	h	y
g	i	z	b	w	i	t	c	h	l
e	g	l	d	b	e	d	l	e	y
b	l	g	i	r	a	f	f	e	t

1

조깅

2

개구리

3

오르다

4

마녀

5

양배추

6
기린

A (　　) 안에서 알맞은 것을 고르세요.

1 The story (don't / doesn't) sound scary.　그 이야기는 무섭게 들리지 않는다.

2 (Do / Does) you love your brother?　너는 너의 오빠를 사랑하니?

3 She doesn't (work / works) at the school.　그녀는 그 학교에서 일하지 않는다.

4 (Do / Does) he ride his bike on Mondays?　그는 월요일마다 자전거를 타니?

5 Leo (don't / doesn't) play the harp.　Leo는 하프를 연주하지 않는다.

6 The store doesn't (sell / sells) potatoes.　그 가게는 감자를 팔지 않는다.

7 (Do / Does) Ian and Joe hate me?　Ian과 Joe는 나를 싫어하니?

8 I (don't / doesn't) dance very well.　나는 춤을 매우 잘 추지는 않는다.

9 The witch (don't / doesn't) tell the truth.　그 마녀는 진실을 말하지 않는다.

10 A: (Do / Does) the earth go around the sun?　지구는 태양 주위를 도니?
　　 B: Yes, it (do / does).　응, 그래.

11 A: (Do / Does) they work this week?　그들은 이번 주에 일하니?
　　 B: No, they (do / don't).　아니, 그렇지 않아.

B 우리말과 같은 뜻이 되도록 보기 에서 알맞은 단어를 골라 대화를 완성하세요.

> 보기   cook   hurt   know   go   like   play   climb

1 A: 그들은 치과에 가니? / B: 응, 그래.

→ A: ______________ ______________ ______________ to the dentist?

B: Yes, ______________ ______________.

2 A: 그는 슬픈 영화를 좋아하니? / B: 아니, 그렇지 않아.

→ A: ______________ ______________ ______________ sad movies?

B: No, ______________ ______________.

3 A: 너는 내 주소를 알고 있니? / B: 아니, 그렇지 않아.

→ A: ______________ ______________ ______________ my address?

B: No, I ______________.

4 A: 너의 머리가 아프니? / B: 응, 그래.

→ A: ______________ your head ______________?

B: Yes, ______________ ______________.

5 A: 그녀는 기타를 연주하니? / B: 응, 그래.

→ A: ______________ ______________ ______________ the guitar?

B: Yes, ______________ ______________.

6 A: 너희는 저녁을 요리하니? / B: 아니, 그렇지 않아.

→ A: ______________ ______________ ______________ dinner?

B: No, we ______________.

7 A: 원숭이들은 나무를 오르니? / B: 응, 그래.

→ A: ______________ monkeys ______________ trees?

B: Yes, ______________ ______________.

A 빈칸에 알맞은 말을 써서 부정문으로 바꾸세요.

1 They like horror movies.   그들은 무서운 영화를 좋아한다.

→ They ______________ ______________ horror movies.

2 Bell has black hair.   Bell은 검은 머리를 가지고 있다.

→ Bell ______________ ______________ black hair.

3 Those dancers jump high.   저 무용수들은 높이 점프한다.

→ Those dancers ______________ ______________ high.

4 The show starts at 4:00 p.m.   그 쇼는 오후 4시에 시작한다.

→ The show ______________ ______________ at 4:00 p.m.

5 The apple juice tastes bitter.   그 사과 주스는 쓴 맛이 난다.

→ The apple juice ______________ ______________ bitter.

6 Irene exercises every day.   Irene은 매일 운동한다.

→ Irene ______________ ______________ every day.

7 She tells lies.   그녀는 거짓말을 한다.

→ She ______________ ______________ lies.

8 We know each other.   우리는 서로 안다.

→ We ______________ ______________ each other.

9 I eat carrots.   나는 당근을 먹는다.

→ I ______________ ______________ carrots.

10 It looks fun.   그것은 재미있어 보인다.

→ It ______________ ______________ fun.

B 빈칸에 알맞은 말을 써서 의문문으로 바꾸세요.

1 She drinks coffee. 그녀는 커피를 마신다.

→ _____________ _____________ _____________ coffee?

2 They play football after school. 그들은 방과 후에 풋볼을 한다.

→ _____________ _____________ _____________ football after school?

3 He wants some more milk. 그는 우유를 좀 더 원한다.

→ _____________ _____________ _____________ some more milk?

4 Andy gets up late in the morning. Andy는 아침에 늦게 일어난다.

→ _____________ _____________ _____________ up late in the morning?

5 We need spoons and forks. 우리는 숟가락과 포크가 필요하다.

→ _____________ _____________ _____________ spoons and forks?

6 People look happy here. 사람들은 이곳에서 행복해 보인다.

→ _____________ _____________ _____________ happy here?

7 Kate helps poor people. Kate는 불쌍한 사람들을 돕는다.

→ _____________ _____________ _____________ poor people?

8 The bookstore sells magazines. 그 서점은 잡지들을 판다.

→ _____________ _____________ _____________ magazines?

9 Tiffany has an aunt. Tiffany는 이모가 있다.

→ _____________ _____________ _____________ an aunt?

10 Emily and Dan fight every day. Emily와 Dan은 매일 싸운다.

→ _____________ _____________ _____________ _____________ every day?

A 주어진 동사를 알맞은 현재형으로 쓰고, 주어진 지시대로 문장을 바꿔 쓸 때 빈칸에 알맞은 말을 쓰세요.

1 I _____________ to school by subway. (go)

나는 학교에 지하철을 타고 간다.

➡ I _____________ _____________ to school by subway. (부정문)

2 Nick _____________ _____________ at 7:00 a.m. (get up)

Nick은 오전 7시에 일어난다.

➡ _____________ _____________ _____________ _____________ at 7:00 a.m.? (의문문)

3 Her sister _____________ French. (study)

그녀의 여동생은 프랑스어를 공부한다.

➡ Her sister _____________ _____________ French. (부정문)

4 They _____________ a test today. (have)

그들은 오늘 시험을 본다.

➡ They _____________ _____________ a test today. (부정문)

5 Giraffes _____________ leaves. (eat)

기린들은 나뭇잎들을 먹는다.

➡ _____________ _____________ _____________ leaves? (의문문)

6 It _____________ at 8:00 a.m. (start)

그것은 오전 8시에 시작한다.

➡ _____________ _____________ _____________ at 8:00 a.m.? (의문문)

B 밑줄 친 부분을 바르게 고쳐 문장을 다시 쓰세요. (부정문은 축약형으로 쓰세요.)

1 Koalas <u>doesn't</u> eat fish.　코알라들은 생선을 먹지 않는다.

→ ____

2 My dogs don't <u>barks</u> at all.　내 개들은 전혀 짖지 않는다.

→ ____

3 <u>Does</u> they raise goats?　그들은 염소들을 키우니?

→ ____

4 <u>Do</u> water freeze at 100°C?　물은 섭씨 100도에서 어니?

→ ____

5 The monster doesn't <u>has</u> a big mouth.　그 괴물은 큰 입을 가지고 있지 않다.

→ ____

6 <u>Does</u> you watch TV at night?　너는 밤에 TV를 보니?

→ ____

7 We <u>doesn't</u> need a small bowl.　우리는 작은 그릇이 필요하지 않다.

→ ____

8 <u>Does</u> your parents have a car?　네 부모님은 차를 가지고 있으시니?

→ ____

9 My friend <u>don't</u> like cloudy days.　내 친구는 흐린 날들을 좋아하지 않는다.

→ ____

10 <u>Do</u> the movie end at 5:00 p.m.?　그 영화는 오후 5시에 끝나니?

→ ____

A 우리말과 같은 뜻이 되도록 주어진 말을 이용하여 문장을 완성하세요.

1 그녀는 캐나다에 사니? (live)

➡ ______________ ______________ ______________ in Canada?

2 그는 매일 밤 책을 읽지 않는다. (read)

➡ ______________ ______________ ______________ a book every night.

3 그들은 일이 끝난 후에 운동하지 않는다. (exercise)

➡ ______________ ______________ ______________ after work.

4 이 담요는 부드럽게 느껴지니? (feel)

➡ ______________ this blanket ______________ soft?

5 그 기차는 오전 4시 30분에 떠나지 않는다. (leave)

➡ The train ______________ ______________ at 4:30 a.m.

6 곰들은 겨울 내내 자니? (sleep)

➡ ______________ bears ______________ all winter?

7 내 양말은 깨끗해 보이지 않는다. (look)

➡ My socks ______________ ______________ clean.

8 이 남자들은 답을 알고 있니? (know)

➡ ______________ these men ______________ the answer?

9 네 남동생은 야구를 하니? (play)

→ ______________ your brother ______________ baseball?

10 우리는 초콜릿 케이크를 좋아하지 않는다. (like)

→ ______________ ______________ ______________ chocolate cake.

11 Jessica는 Emma를 신뢰하지 않는다. (trust)

→ Jessica ______________ ______________ Emma.

12 Eric은 일이 끝난 후에 운동하니? (exercise)

→ ______________________________________

13 그들은 캐나다에 살지 않는다. (live)

→ ______________________________________

14 나는 매일 밤 신문을 읽지 않는다. (the newspaper)

→ ______________________________________

15 이 베개는 부드럽게 느껴지지 않는다. (pillow)

→ ______________________________________

16 그녀는 초콜릿 케이크를 좋아하니? (like)

→ ______________________________________

17 우리는 농구를 하지 않는다. (play, basketball)

→ ______________________________________

A 다음 단어를 두 번씩 듣고 따라 쓴 후 그 뜻을 쓰세요.

단어	두 번 따라 쓰기	뜻 쓰기
excited 신이 난		
interesting 흥미로운		
street 거리, 도로		
nervous 긴장한		
scientist 과학자		
busy 바쁜		
zoo 동물원		
boring 지루한		
fresh 신선한		
department store 백화점		
tasty 맛있는		
scary 무서운		
sweet 달콤한		

단어	두 번 따라 쓰기	뜻 쓰기
amusement park 놀이공원		
theater 극장		
thirsty 목이 마른		
salty 짠, 짭짤한		
weather 날씨		
brave 용감한		
army 군대		
refrigerator 냉장고		
expensive 비싼		
surprised 놀란		
shelf 선반		
confident 자신감 있는		
tray 쟁반		

A 주어진 철자의 순서를 바르게 맞추어 우리말 뜻에 해당하는 단어를 쓰세요.

1 
ozo
동물원

2 
torgerafrire
냉장고

3 
ttyshir
목이 마른

4 
etews
달콤한

5 
denconfit
자신감 있는

6 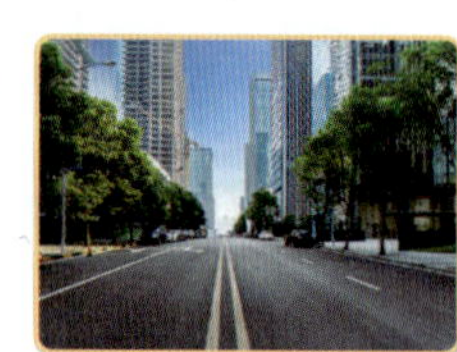
eesttr
거리, 도로

B 우리말과 같은 뜻이 되도록 보기 에서 알맞은 단어를 골라 쓰세요.

보기   weather   interesting   salty   brave   surprised

1 It was an ______________ movie.   그것은 흥미로운 영화였다.

2 The little girl was ______________.   그 작은 소녀는 용감했다.

3 We were ______________ at the news.   우리는 그 소식에 놀랐다.

4 The pizza was ______________.   피자는 짰다.

5 The ______________ was very nice.   날씨가 무척 좋았다.

C 다음 사진에 해당하는 단어를 아래 퍼즐에서 찾아 ◯ 표시하고 빈칸에 쓰세요.

s	p	f	l	l	d	w	e	r	q
n	e	r	v	o	u	s	s	o	y
n	j	e	s	y	u	c	e	w	v
a	h	s	r	k	r	i	u	e	e
r	g	h	p	s	h	e	l	f	s
m	i	e	b	p	l	n	u	p	l
y	g	l	d	h	e	t	r	a	y
s	c	i	e	n	t	i	s	t	t

1 긴장한

2 군대

3 신선한

4 과학자

5 선반

6 쟁반

A ( ) 안에서 알맞은 것을 고르세요.

1 The tray (was / were) on the table. 그 쟁반은 테이블 위에 있었다.

2 My cats (are / were) sick last week. 지난주에 내 고양이들이 아팠다.

3 Sarah (is / was) a writer a few years ago. Sarah는 몇 년 전에 작가였다.

4 I (am / was) at the amusement park right now. 나는 지금 놀이공원에 있다.

5 The boys (was / were) thirsty last night. 그 소년들은 어젯밤에 목이 말랐다.

6 She (is / was) happy now. 그녀는 지금 행복하다.

7 The doctors (was / were) in Africa in 2010. 그 의사들은 2010년에 아프리카에 있었다.

8 They (are / were) at the police station now. 그들은 지금 경찰서에 있다.

9 He (was / were) very nervous. 그는 매우 긴장했었다.

10 My sister (is / was) in China before. 나의 언니는 전에 중국에 있었다.

11 They (are / were) at the restaurant an hour ago. 그들은 한 시간 전에 식당에 있었다.

12 Yesterday (is / was) cold. 어제는 추웠다.

B 빈칸에 알맞은 be동사의 과거형을 쓰세요.

1 The man ____________ a hockey player. 그 남자는 하키 선수였다.

2 They ____________ in the department store. 그들은 백화점에 있었다.

3 I ____________ 10 years old at that time. 나는 그 당시에 10살이었다.

4 The movie ____________ scary. 그 영화는 무서웠다.

5 The milk ____________ fresh yesterday. 어제 그 우유는 신선했다.

6 Her socks ____________ in the box. 그녀의 양말은 상자 안에 있었다.

7 We ____________ classmates last year. 우리는 작년에 같은 반이었다.

8 The keys ____________ under the sofa. 그 열쇠들은 소파 아래에 있었다.

9 It ____________ my favorite toy. 그것은 내가 가장 좋아하는 장난감이었다.

10 Red flowers ____________ in my garden. 빨간 꽃들이 나의 정원에 있었다.

11 The food ____________ warm. 그 음식은 따뜻했다.

12 These comic books ____________ popular. 이 만화책들은 인기 있었다.

A ( ) 안에서 알맞은 be동사를 고르고, 과거시제로 바꿔 쓰세요.

1 They (am / are / is) great soccer players. 그들은 훌륭한 축구 선수들이다.

→ They ______________ great soccer players.

2 The puppies (am / are / is) in the woods. 강아지들은 숲속에 있다.

→ The puppies ______________ in the woods.

3 The necklace (am / are / is) my mom's. 그 목걸이는 나의 엄마의 것이다.

→ The necklace ______________ my mom's.

4 I (am / are / is) a teacher. 나는 선생님이다.

→ I ______________ a teacher.

5 The two boys (am / are / is) roommates. 두 소년들은 룸메이트이다.

→ The two boys ______________ roommates.

6 Your notebooks (am / are / is) on the desk. 너의 공책들은 책상 위에 있다.

→ Your notebooks ______________ on the desk.

7 The wolves (am / are / is) in the cage. 늑대들은 우리 안에 있다.

→ The wolves ______________ in the cage.

8 The steak (am / are / is) salty. 그 스테이크는 짜다.

→ The steak ______________ salty.

9 The orange juice (am / are / is) in the refrigerator. 그 오렌지 주스는 냉장고 안에 있다.

→ The Orange juice ______________ in the refrigerator.

10 The movie tickets (am / are / is) expensive. 그 영화 티켓들은 비싸다.

→ The movie tickets ______________ expensive.

B 다음 문장을 주어진 주어로 시작하는 문장으로 바꿔 쓰세요.

1 Sarah and Anna were neighbors last year.　Sarah와 Anna는 작년에 이웃이었다.

→ We _______________________________________.

2 She was a guitarist at that time.　그녀는 그 당시에 기타 연주자였다.

→ My uncle _______________________________________.

3 My cat was on the bed last night.　나의 고양이는 어젯밤에 침대 위에 있었다.

→ The bag _______________________________________.

4 I was at the mall the day before yesterday.　나는 그저께 쇼핑몰에 있었다.

→ My mom _______________________________________.

5 His room was clean yesterday morning.　그의 방은 어제 아침에 깨끗했다.

→ The offices _______________________________________.

6 The new game was fun.　그 새로운 게임은 재미있었다.

→ His stories _______________________________________.

7 The boys were best friends before.　그 소년들은 전에 단짝 친구였다.

→ Jake and I _______________________________________.

8 The water was very cold an hour ago.　한 시간 전에 물이 매우 차가웠다.

→ The milk _______________________________________.

9 My puppies were sick last month.　내 강아지들이 지난달에 아팠다.

→ The kid _______________________________________.

10 The men were famous artists before.　그 남자들은 전에 유명한 화가들이었다.

→ They _______________________________________.

A 우리말과 같은 뜻이 되도록 보기 에서 알맞은 단어를 골라 문장을 완성하세요.

| 보기 | small | busy | sweet | nervous | surprised |
| | clean | happy | sunny | tasty | boring |

1 The girl ______________ ______________ by the gift yesterday.

그 소녀는 어제 그 선물에 놀랐다.

2 The ice cream ______________ ______________.

그 아이스크림은 맛있었다.

3 The boxes ______________ ______________.

그 상자들은 작았다.

4 His desk ______________ ______________.

그의 책상은 깨끗했다.

5 She ______________ ______________ now.

그녀는 지금 행복하다.

6 It ______________ ______________ on Saturday.

토요일은 날씨가 맑았다.

7 We ______________ ______________ at that time.

우리는 그 당시에 긴장했다.

8 They ______________ ______________ right now.

그들은 지금 바쁘다.

9 The cookies ______________ ______________.

그 쿠키들은 달콤했다.

10 The festival ______________ ______________.

그 축제는 지루했다.

B 밑줄 친 부분을 바르게 고쳐 문장을 다시 쓰세요.

1 Those <u>was</u> my favorite dolls.   저것들은 내가 가장 좋아하는 인형들이었다.

→ ____

2 The street <u>were</u> very dirty.   그 거리는 매우 지저분했다.

→ ____

3 We <u>are</u> students at that time.   우리는 그 당시에 학생이었다.

→ ____

4 The living room <u>were</u> dirty an hour ago.   거실은 한 시간 전에 더러웠다.

→ ____

5 I <u>am</u> a singer 10 years ago.   나는 10년 전에 가수였다.

→ ____

6 It <u>were</u> a boring book.   그것은 지루한 책이었다.

→ ____

7 They <u>are</u> elementary school students in 2020.   그들은 2020년에 초등학생들이었다.

→ ____

8 The elephants <u>was</u> in the zoo.   그 코끼리들은 동물원에 있었다.

→ ____

9 My brother <u>is</u> hungry last night.   나의 남동생은 어젯밤에 배가 고팠다.

→ ____

10 The waiters <u>was</u> very busy yesterday.   웨이터들은 어제 매우 바빴다.

→ ____

A 우리말과 같은 뜻이 되도록 주어진 말을 이용하여 문장을 완성하세요.

1 그 손목시계는 나의 할머니의 것이었다. (watch)

➡ The ＿＿＿＿＿＿ ＿＿＿＿＿＿ my grandmother's.

2 그 책들은 책상 위에 있었다. (books)

➡ The ＿＿＿＿＿＿ ＿＿＿＿＿＿ on the desk.

3 그 아이들은 모두에게 친절했다. (kind)

➡ The kids ＿＿＿＿＿＿ ＿＿＿＿＿＿ to everyone.

4 Anna는 그 당시에 자신감이 있었다. (confident)

➡ Anna ＿＿＿＿＿＿ ＿＿＿＿＿＿ at that time.

5 어제 날씨가 좋았다. (good)

➡ The weather ＿＿＿＿＿＿ ＿＿＿＿＿＿ yesterday.

6 그녀는 어젯밤에 매우 피곤했다. (tired)

➡ She ＿＿＿＿＿＿ very ＿＿＿＿＿＿ last night.

7 그들은 선물들에 신이 났었다. (excited)

➡ They ＿＿＿＿＿＿ ＿＿＿＿＿＿ about the gifts.

8 어제 바람이 불었다. (windy)

➡ It ＿＿＿＿＿＿ ＿＿＿＿＿＿ yesterday.

9 방안의 바닥이 깨끗했다. (clean)

➡ The floor _____________ _____________ in the room.

10 나의 엄마는 전에 의사였다. (a doctor)

➡ My mom _____________ _____________ _____________ before.

11 그 나뭇잎들은 한 달 전에 초록색이었다. (leaves)

➡ The _____________ _____________ green a month ago.

12 그 연필은 책상 위에 있었다. (the pencil)

➡ ____

13 그 안경은 Peter의 것이었다. (the glasses)

➡ ____

14 우리는 그 당시에 자신감이 있었다. (confident)

➡ ____

15 그는 우리에게 친절했다. (kind)

➡ ____

16 그들은 전에 의사였다. (doctors)

➡ ____

17 Cathy는 선물들에 신이 났다. (excited)

➡ ____

A 다음 단어를 두 번씩 듣고 따라 쓴 후 그 뜻을 쓰세요.

단어	두 번 따라 쓰기		뜻 쓰기
rude 무례한			
difficult 어려운			
absent 결석한			
heavy 무거운			
beach 해변, 바닷가			
comic book 만화책			
alone 혼자			
hospital 병원			
delicious 맛있는			
comfortable 편안한			
polite 공손한			
wallet 지갑			
meeting 회의			

단어	두 번 따라 쓰기		뜻 쓰기
light 가벼운			
colorful (색이) 다채로운			
roof 지붕			
comedian 코미디언			
animal 동물			
director 감독			
train 기차			
cheap 저렴한			
audience 관객			

A 주어진 철자의 순서를 바르게 맞추어 우리말 뜻에 해당하는 단어를 쓰세요.

1  etmiegn
회의

2  licideous
맛있는

3  inatr
기차

4  ablecomtorf
편안한

5  diceenau
관객

6  mniala
동물

B 우리말과 같은 뜻이 되도록 보기 에서 알맞은 단어를 골라 쓰세요.

보기   comic book   cheap   polite   director   difficult

1 The math test was ______________.   수학 시험은 어려웠다.

2 The ______________ was interesting.   그 만화책은 재미있었다.

3 The kids are ______________.   그 아이들은 공손하다.

4 He wants to be a ______________ someday.   그는 언젠가 감독이 되고 싶어 한다.

5 These shoes were very ______________.   이 신발은 무척 저렴했다.

C 다음 사진에 해당하는 단어를 아래 퍼즐에서 찾아 ○ 표시하고 빈칸에 쓰세요.

s	b	e	a	c	h	w	e	w	c
h	r	c	f	x	t	c	s	a	l
e	h	o	s	p	i	t	a	l	a
a	a	t	e	r	r	e	l	l	n
v	i	o	n	e	o	k	g	e	s
y	m	s	g	p	o	c	u	t	h
c	o	l	o	r	f	u	l	b	e
n	o	i	e	o	g	e	l	e	m

1 
해변, 바닷가

2 
병원

3 
지갑

4 
(색이) 다채로운

5
지붕

6
무거운

A (　) 안에서 알맞은 것을 고르세요.

1 The shoes (was / were) not small for him.　그 신발은 그에게 작지 않았다.

2 (Was / Were) she in Paris in 2019?　그녀는 2019년에 파리에 있었니?

3 (Was / Were) the actors famous before?　그 배우들은 전에 유명했니?

4 She (wasn't / weren't) a designer at that time.　그녀는 그 당시에 디자이너가 아니었다.

5 The boy (was not / were not) smart.　그 소년은 똑똑하지 않았다.

6 The birds (wasn't / weren't) in a tree.　그 새들은 나무에 있지 않았다.

7 (Was / Were) you late for the meeting this morning?
너는 오늘 아침에 회의에 늦었니?

8 (Was / Were) James a basketball player two years ago?
James는 2년 전에 농구 선수였니?

9 (Was / Were) the food great there?　그곳의 음식은 훌륭했니?

10 I (wasn't / weren't) tired last night.　나는 어젯밤에 피곤하지 않았다.

11 The vegetables (was / were) not fresh last week.
그 채소들은 지난주에 신선하지 않았다.

12 Sarah and Jim (wasn't / weren't) in the same class.
Sarah와 Jim은 같은 반이 아니었다.

B 빈칸에 알맞은 be동사의 과거형을 쓰세요.

1 ______________ they soccer players?　그들은 축구 선수들이었니?

2 She ______________ not an artist before.　그녀는 전에 화가가 아니었다.

3 ______________ the kids happy?　그 아이들은 행복했니?

4 My parents ______________ not at home last weekend.
나의 부모님은 지난 주말에 집에 계시지 않았다.

5 ______________ you at the beach?　너는 바닷가에 있었니?

6 Dan ______________ not 12 years old last year.　Dan은 작년에 12살이 아니었다.

7 ______________ the actor popular before?　그 배우는 전에 인기가 있었니?

8 ______________ the waiters kind to you?　웨이터들은 너에게 친절했니?

9 ______________ they at the bank?　그들은 은행에 있었니?

10 The musical ______________ not funny.　그 뮤지컬은 재미있지 않았다.

11 The weather ______________ not bad yesterday.　어제 날씨는 나쁘지 않았다.

12 ______________ the bread delicious?　그 빵은 맛있었니?

A 빈칸에 알맞은 be동사의 과거형을 쓰고, 축약형을 사용하여 부정문으로 바꾸세요.

1 We ___________ busy yesterday.　우리는 어제 바빴다.

→ We ___________ busy yesterday.　우리는 어제 바쁘지 않았다.

2 She ___________ alone then.　그녀는 그때 혼자였다.

→ She ___________ alone then.　그녀는 그때 혼자가 아니었다.

3 The kids ___________ in the hospital last week.

그 아이들은 지난주에 병원에 있었다.

→ The kids ___________ in the hospital last week.

그 아이들은 지난주에 병원에 있지 않았다.

4 The science test ___________ easy.　과학 시험은 쉬웠다.

→ The science test ___________ easy.　과학 시험은 쉽지 않았다.

5 His mom ___________ angry at him.　그의 엄마는 그에게 화가 나셨다.

→ His mom ___________ angry at him.　그의 엄마는 그에게 화가 나지 않으셨다.

6 They ___________ in Seoul last week.　그들은 지난주에 서울에 있었다.

→ They ___________ in Seoul last week.　그들은 지난주에 서울에 있지 않았다.

7 The movie ___________ boring.　그 영화는 지루했다.

→ The movie ___________ boring.　그 영화는 지루하지 않았다.

8 The shirts ___________ my brother's.　그 셔츠들은 내 형의 것이었다.

→ The shirts ___________ my brother's.　그 셔츠들은 내 형의 것이 아니었다.

9 The pasta ___________ warm enough.　그 파스타는 충분히 따뜻했다.

→ The pasta ___________ warm enough.　그 파스타는 충분히 따뜻하지 않았다.

10 It ___________ cloudy in Seoul yesterday.　어제 서울은 흐렸다.

→ It ___________ cloudy in Seoul yesterday.　어제 서울은 흐리지 않았다.

B 빈칸에 알맞은 말을 써서 의문문으로 바꾸세요.

1 The weather was warm yesterday.   어제 날씨는 따뜻했다.

→ ___________________________ warm yesterday?   어제 날씨는 따뜻했니?

2 The bags were old.   그 가방들은 낡았었다.

→ ___________________________ old?   그 가방들은 낡았었니?

3 She was in Italy in 2019.   그녀는 2019년에 이탈리아에 있었다.

→ ___________________________ in Italy in 2019?   그녀는 2019년에 이탈리아에 있었니?

4 They were basketball players.   그들은 농구 선수들이었다.

→ ___________________________ basketball players?   그들은 농구 선수들이었니?

5 The test was difficult.   그 시험은 어려웠다.

→ ___________________________ difficult?   그 시험은 어려웠니?

6 Jim was absent from school yesterday.   Jim은 어제 학교에 결석했다.

→ ___________________________ absent from school yesterday?

Jim은 어제 학교에 결석했니?

7 The new sofa was comfortable.   새 소파는 편안했다.

→ ___________________________ comfortable?   새 소파는 편안했니?

8 The writer was popular before.   그 작가는 전에 인기가 있었다.

→ ___________________________ popular before?   그 작가는 전에 인기가 있었니?

9 The tables were clean this morning.   오늘 아침에 탁자들이 깨끗했다.

→ ___________________________ clean this morning?   오늘 아침에 탁자들이 깨끗했니?

10 The students were on the train.   학생들은 기차에 타고 있었다.

→ ___________________________ on the train?   학생들은 기차에 타고 있었니?

A 우리말과 같은 뜻이 되도록 주어진 말을 바르게 배열하세요.

1 그들은 그 당시에 영어를 잘했니? (good at English / they / were)

→ ____ at that time?

2 그 토마토들은 신선하지 않았다. (not / the tomatoes / fresh / were)

→ ____.

3 그 책상은 무거웠니? (the desk / heavy / was)

→ ____?

4 그 꽃들은 색이 다채롭지 않았다. (colorful / the flowers / weren't)

→ ____.

5 저 예술가들은 전에 배우들이었니? (actors / those artists / were)

→ ____ before?

6 어제 눈이 왔니? (it / snowy / was)

→ ____ yesterday?

7 그 책들은 비싸지 않았다. (not / the books / expensive / were)

→ ____.

8 나는 2년 전에 야구 선수가 아니었다. (I / a baseball player / not / was)

→ ____ two years ago.

9 그의 새 책은 흥미로웠니? (his / was / interesting / new book)

→ ____?

10 그는 수학 선생님이 아니었다. (a math teacher / was / not / he)

→ ____.

B 밑줄 친 부분을 바르게 고쳐 문장을 다시 쓰세요. (부정문은 축약형으로 쓰세요.)

1 The students <u>wasn't</u> late for the class.　학생들은 수업에 지각하지 않았다.

　➞ ____

2 <u>Was</u> you at home last night?　너는 어젯밤에 집에 있었니?

　➞ ____

3 The chair <u>weren't</u> light.　그 의자는 가볍지 않았다.

　➞ ____

4 They <u>wasn't</u> polite to their teacher.　그들은 선생님께 공손하지 않았다.

　➞ ____

5 <u>Were</u> your room clean yesterday?　네 방은 어제 깨끗했니?

　➞ ____

6 <u>Were</u> the food delicious there?　그곳의 음식은 맛있었니?

　➞ ____

7 We <u>was not</u> in Jeju-do yesterday.　우리는 어제 제주도에 있지 않았다.

　➞ ____

8 <u>Was</u> their stories boring?　그들의 이야기들이 지루했니?

　➞ ____

9 <u>Was</u> you at the museum?　너희들은 박물관에 있었니?

　➞ ____

10 It <u>weren't</u> snowy in Busan last winter.　지난 겨울에 부산에는 눈이 내리지 않았다.

　➞ ____

A 우리말과 같은 뜻이 되도록 주어진 말을 이용하여 문장을 완성하세요.

1 그 감독들은 전에 유명하지 않았다. (famous)

➡ The directors ______________ ______________ before.

2 그 영화는 흥미로웠니? (interesting)

➡ ______________ the movie ______________?

3 어제는 눈이 내리지 않았다. (snowy)

➡ It ______________ ______________ yesterday.

4 그 거북이들은 해변에 있지 않았다. (turtles)

➡ The ______________ ______________ on the beach.

5 그 아이들은 학교에 결석했니? (the kids)

➡ ______________ ______________ ______________ absent from school?

6 너의 부모님은 한 시간 전에 이곳에 계셨니? / 아니, 그러지 않으셨어. (your parents)

➡ A: ______________ ______________ ______________ here an hour ago?

B: No, ______________ ______________.

7 너는 도서관에 있었니? / 응, 그랬어. (you)

➡ A: ______________ ______________ at the library?

B: Yes, I ______________.

8 그 책은 네 책상 위에 없었다. (book)

➡ The ______________ ______________ on your desk.

9 Tom은 2년 전에 야구 선수였니? (Tom)

→ ______________ ______________ a baseball player two years ago?

10 나의 코치는 지난주에 바쁘지 않았다. (busy)

→ My coach ______________ ______________ last week.

11 그 동물들은 건강했니? (healthy)

→ ______________ the animals ______________?

12 Julia는 학교에 결석했니? (absent from school)

→ ____

13 너의 고양이는 건강했니? (your cat)

→ ____

14 그 가수는 전에 유명하지 않았다. (the singer)

→ ____

15 그 만화책들은 네 책상 위에 없었다. (the comic books)

→ ____

16 그들은 지난주에 바쁘지 않았다. (busy)

→ ____

17 그 남자는 해변에 있지 않았다. (the man)

→ ____

A 다음 단어를 두 번씩 듣고 따라 쓴 후 그 뜻을 쓰세요.

단어	두 번 따라 쓰기	뜻 쓰기
toothbrush 칫솔		
basket 바구니		
hill 언덕		
farm 농장		
cupboard 찬장		
vase 꽃병		
subway 지하철		
customer 고객		
tourist 관광객		
palace 궁전		
drawer 서랍		
playground 놀이터		
theater 극장		

단어	두 번 따라 쓰기	뜻 쓰기
holiday 휴일		
plate 접시		
pond 연못		
downtown 시내		
closet 옷장		
dust 먼지		
plant 식물		
insect 곤충		
ladder 사다리		
fishbowl 어항		
clothes 옷		
trash can 쓰레기통		
island 섬		

A 주어진 철자의 순서를 바르게 맞추어 우리말 뜻에 해당하는 단어를 쓰세요.

1  ketsab
바구니

2  lscoet
옷장

3  alntp
식물

4  dadelr
사다리

5  radrwe
서랍

6 thbrsuhtoo
칫솔

B 우리말과 같은 뜻이 되도록 보기 에서 알맞은 단어를 골라 쓰세요.

보기　cupboard　farm　fishbowl　island　theater

1 There is a beautiful ________________. 아름다운 섬이 있다.

2 There was a fish in the ________________. 어항에 물고기 한 마리가 있었다.

3 Are there plates in the ________________? 찬장 안에 접시들이 있니?

4 There were many animals on the ________________. 농장에 많은 동물들이 있었다.

5 Jake went to the ________________ last Sunday. Jake는 지난 일요일에 극장에 갔다.

C 다음 사진에 해당하는 단어를 아래 퍼즐에서 찾아 ○ 표시하고 빈칸에 쓰세요.

s	p	c	u	s	t	o	m	e	r
i	b	l	m	b	o	o	s	o	u
n	p	o	n	d	i	n	g	p	i
a	h	t	r	i	g	h	u	a	p
e	g	h	p	a	e	w	k	l	u
k	i	e	b	s	u	b	w	a	y
v	a	s	e	n	e	d	l	c	o
a	l	s	t	a	f	e	l	e	t

1 옷

2 연못

3 고객

4 꽃병

5 지하철

6 궁전

A (   ) 안에서 알맞은 것을 고르세요.

1 There (is / are) a French restaurant downtown.   시내에 프랑스 식당이 있다.

2 (Is / Are) there a baseball stadium in this town?   이 도시에는 야구 경기장이 있니?

3 (Was / Were) there many bikes on the street?   거리에 자전거들이 많이 있었니?

4 There (was / were) houses on this mountain before.   전에 이 산에는 집들이 있었다.

5 (Was / Were) there a basketball team in this school?
이 학교에는 농구팀이 있었니?

6 There (was / were) a smartphone under the sofa.   소파 아래에 스마트폰이 있었다.

7 There (wasn't / weren't) any monkeys in the zoo.   동물원에 원숭이들이 전혀 없었다.

8 There (is / are) toys in my room.   내 방에 장난감들이 있다.

9 There (isn't / aren't) any money in my wallet.   내 지갑 속에는 돈이 전혀 없다.

10 There (isn't / aren't) any toothbrushes in the bathroom.
화장실에 칫솔들이 전혀 없다.

11 (Was / Were) there elephants in the zoo?   동물원에 코끼리들이 있었니?

12 There (was / were) a painting on the wall.   벽에 그림이 하나 있었다.

B 우리말과 같은 뜻이 되도록 빈칸에 알맞은 be동사를 쓰고, 의문문으로 바꿔 쓰세요.

1 There _____________ two rainbows in the sky.   하늘에 두 개의 무지개가 있다.

➡ _____________ _____________ two rainbows in the sky?

2 There _____________ a hamster in the cage.   우리 안에 햄스터 한 마리가 있었다.

➡ _____________ _____________ a hamster in the cage?

3 There _____________ a movie poster on the wall.   벽에 영화 포스터가 하나 있다.

➡ _____________ _____________ a movie poster on the wall?

4 There _____________ yogurt in the bowl.   그릇 안에 요거트가 있었다.

➡ _____________ _____________ yogurt in the bowl?

5 There _____________ many books on the desk.   책상 위에 많은 책들이 있었다.

➡ _____________ _____________ many books on the desk?

6 There _____________ ice in the cup.   컵 안에 얼음이 있다.

➡ _____________ _____________ ice in the cup?

7 There _____________ tomatoes in the refrigerator.   냉장고 안에 토마토들이 있다.

➡ _____________ _____________ tomatoes in the refrigerator?

8 There _____________ many sheep on the hill.   언덕 위에 많은 양들이 있었다.

➡ _____________ _____________ many sheep on the hill?

9 There _____________ children at the amusement park.   놀이공원에 아이들이 있다.

➡ _____________ _____________ children at the amusement park?

10 There _____________ fruit juice in the cup.   컵 안에 과일 주스가 있었다.

➡ _____________ _____________ fruit juice in the cup?

A 우리말과 같은 뜻이 되도록 주어진 말을 바르게 배열하세요.

1 해변에 쓰레기통이 하나 있었다. (was / a trash can / there)

→ ______________________________________ on the beach.

2 공원에는 사람들이 많이 없다. (are / there / not / many people)

→ ______________________________________ in the park.

3 어제 아침에 바닷가에 아이들이 있었다. (kids / there / were)

→ ______________________________ on the beach yesterday morning.

4 여기 근처에 좋은 식당이 있니? (there / a good restaurant / is)

→ ______________________________________ near here?

5 새장 안에 새 두 마리가 있었다. (two / there / birds / were)

→ ______________________________________ in the cage.

6 나의 마을에는 백화점이 없다. (not / a department store / there / is)

→ ______________________________________ in my town.

7 길 건너편에 은행이 있었니? (was / a bank / there)

→ ______________________________________ across the street?

8 그 섬에는 많은 관광객들이 있었다. (there / many tourists / were)

→ ______________________________________ on the island.

9 소파 아래에는 신발이 전혀 없었다. (not / any shoes / were / there)

→ ______________________________________ under the sofa.

10 여기 근처에 지하철역이 있니? (there / a subway station / is)

→ ______________________________________ near here?

B 우리말과 같은 뜻이 되도록 빈칸에 알맞은 말을 넣어 대화를 완성하세요.

1 A: ______________ there scissors on the desk? 책상 위에 가위가 있니?

 B: No, ______________ ______________. 아니, 없어.

2 A: ______________ there tea in the cupboard? 찬장 안에 차가 있니?

 B: No, ______________ ______________. 아니, 없어.

3 A: ______________ there dolphins in the zoo? 동물원에 돌고래들이 있었니?

 B: No, ______________ ______________. 아니, 없었어.

4 A: ______________ there students in the classroom? 교실에 학생들이 있니?

 B: Yes, ______________ ______________. 응, 있어.

5 A: ______________ there candles on the cake? 케이크 위에 양초들이 있었니?

 B: Yes, ______________ ______________. 응, 있었어.

6 A: ______________ there a school here before? 이곳에 전에 학교가 있었니?

 B: Yes, ______________ ______________. 응, 있었어.

7 A: ______________ there many clothes in the closet? 옷장 안에 많은 옷들이 있었니?

 B: No, ______________ ______________. 아니, 없었어.

8 A: ______________ there a museum in the town? 그 도시에는 박물관이 있었니?

 B: Yes, ______________ ______________. 응, 있었어.

9 A: ______________ there a closet in the room? 방안에 옷장이 있니?

 B: Yes, ______________ ______________. 응, 있어.

10 A: ______________ there stars in the sky now? 지금 하늘에 별들이 있니?

 B: No, ______________ ______________. 아니, 없어.

A 다음 문장을 주어진 지시대로 바꿔 쓰세요. (부정문은 축약형으로 쓰세요.)

1 There are many trees on this mountain. (부정문)　이 산에는 나무들이 많다.

→ ____

2 There is a laptop on the desk. (의문문)　책상 위에 노트북 컴퓨터가 있다.

→ ____

3 There are many singers at the festival. (과거형)　그 축제에 많은 가수들이 있다.

→ ____

4 There were pigs on the farm. (의문문)　농장에 돼지들이 있었다.

→ ____

5 There is a bank around here. (부정문)　여기 근처에 은행이 있다.

→ ____

6 There were many tourists at the palace. (의문문)　궁전에 많은 관광객들이 있었다.

→ ____

7 There was butter in the refrigerator. (현재형)　냉장고 안에 버터가 있었다.

→ ____

8 There is a mirror on the wall. (과거형)　벽에 거울이 하나 있다.

→ ____

9 There was a baseball team in this school. (의문문)　이 학교에는 야구팀이 있었다.

→ ____

10 There was a wallet in this bag. (현재형)　이 가방 안에 지갑이 하나 있었다.

→ ____

B 우리말과 같은 뜻이 되도록 밑줄 친 부분을 바르게 고쳐 문장을 다시 쓰세요.

1 There <u>was</u> cookies in a bowl.　그릇 안에 쿠키들이 있었다.

→ ____

2 There <u>not are</u> any chairs in the room.　방 안에 의자들이 전혀 없다.

→ ____

3 <u>Was there</u> many customers at the mall?　쇼핑몰에 많은 고객들이 있었니?

→ ____

4 There <u>are</u> pasta on the plate.　접시 위에 파스타가 있다.

→ ____

5 <u>Is</u> there orange juice in the cup?　컵 안에 오렌지주스가 있었니?

→ ____

6 There <u>isn't</u> any flowers on the cake.　케이크 위에 꽃들이 전혀 없다.

→ ____

7 There <u>are</u> two singers on the stage.　무대 위에 두 명의 가수가 있었다.

→ ____

8 There <u>weren't</u> any fish in the fishbowl.　어항에는 물고기들이 전혀 없다.

→ ____

9 There <u>is</u> toys on the floor.　바닥에 장난감들이 있다.

→ ____

10 <u>Was</u> there many holidays last year?　작년에는 휴일들이 많았니?

→ ____

A 우리말과 같은 뜻이 되도록 주어진 말을 이용하여 문장을 완성하세요.

1 여기 근처에 학교가 하나 있다. (a school)

→ ___________ ___________ ___________ ___________ near
here.

2 지붕 위에 사다리가 있었니? (a ladder)

→ ___________ ___________ ___________ ___________ on the
roof?

3 바닥에 카펫이 없다. (a carpet)

→ ___________ ___________ ___________ ___________ on the
floor.

4 찬장 안에 컵들이 있니? (cups)

→ ___________ ___________ ___________ in the cupboard?

5 바구니 안에는 머핀들이 전혀 없었다. (muffins)

→ ___________ ___________ any ___________ in the basket.

6 책상 위에는 식물이 없었다. (a plant)

→ ___________ ___________ ___________ ___________ on the
desk.

7 작년에 많은 축제들이 있었니? (festivals)

→ ___________ ___________ many ___________ last year?

8 접시에 약간의 빵이 있었다. (some bread)

→ ___________ ___________ ___________ ___________ on the
plate.

9 팬에 기름이 있니? (oil)

→ ____________ ____________ __________ in the pan?

10 냉장고 안에 물이 전혀 없었다. (water)

→ ____________ ____________ any __________ in the refrigerator.

11 농장에는 소들이 있었다. (cows)

→ ____________ ____________ __________ on the farm.

12 냉장고 안에 과일이 전혀 없었다. (any fruits)

→ ____

13 여기 근처에 극장이 하나 있다. (a theater)

→ ____

14 접시에 쿠키들이 있었다. (cookies, the plate)

→ ____

15 책상 위에는 많은 펜들이 있었다. (many pens)

→ ____

16 찬장 안에 접시가 있니? (a dish)

→ ____

17 지붕 위에 먼지가 있었니? (dust)

→ ____

MEMO

MEMO

MEMO

초등

Grammar
Inside

Workbook

문법

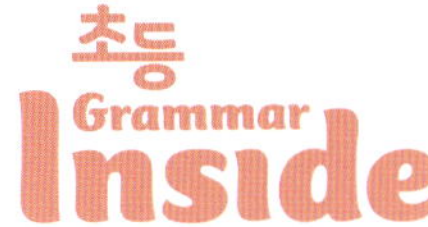

많은 양의 문제를 통해
초등 영문법 기초 다지기
1 | 2 | 3 | 4 | 5 | 6
Grammar Inside

문법을 처음 시작하는
초급 학습자를 위한 문법서
1 | 2 | 3 | 4

GRAMMAR BUDDY

초등학생을 위한 문법 입문서
1 | 2 | 3
Reading Buddy | Listening Buddy

듣기

능률 초등영어
듣기모의고사 10회

초등부터 중등까지!
영어 듣기평가 실전 대비서
4-1 | 4-2 | 5-1 | 5-2 | 6-1 | 6-2

초등영어
LISTENING TUTOR

주제별 표현 학습을 바탕으로
듣기 기초를 다지는 초등 리스닝 기본서
Beginner 1 | Beginner 2 | Beginner 3
Intermediate 1 | Intermediate 2
Intermediate 3

LISTENING BUDDY

초등학생을 위한 리스닝 입문서
1 | 2 | 3
Reading Buddy | Grammar Buddy

예비중 · 중등

문법, 독해, 쓰기, 말하기를
함께 배우는 중학 영어 종합서
예비중 | 중1 | 중2 | 중3

문제로 마스터하는 중학 영문법
Level 1 | Level 2 | Level 3
문마고

GRAMMAR Inside

많은 양의 문제로 체계적으로
학습하는 중학 영문법
Starter | Level 1 | Level 2 | Level 3
Reading Inside

JUNIOR READING EXPERT

앞서가는 중학생들을 위한 원서형 독해 교재
Level 1 | Level 2 | Level 3 | Level 4
Junior Listening Expert |
Reading Expert

능률 중학영어
듣기 모의고사 22회

전국 16개 시·도 교육청 주관
영어듣기평가 실전대비서
Level 1 | Level 2 | Level 3